WEALTH
IN
FAMILIES

THIRD EDITION

Charles W. Collier
Harvard University

ISBN 978-0-615-64827-9
© 2012 President and Fellows of Harvard College
Revised and expanded edition published in 2012

Net proceeds from this book will support financial aid at Harvard University.
This book is available for bulk purchase at a special discount.
For additional information, please call 617-495-1636.

Alumni Affairs and Development Communications/AAD 12-446
Photography: Nick Clements/Photodisc, Martha Stewart '75

This book is dedicated with much love in memory
of my mother and father

Contents

Foreword

When Harvard published the first edition of Charlie Collier's *Wealth in Families* in 2001, the response to the book surprised almost everyone. Based mainly on Charlie's experiences in working with Harvard alumni, *Wealth in Families* had a print run of only a few thousand. The book received little promotion because Harvard planned to give away most of the copies at Charlie's seminars.

Then, something unexpected happened. People began to hear reviews from their colleagues and friends. They called Charlie's office at Harvard to obtain copies. Soon, lawyers and accountants, foundation staff and families themselves were searching for the book. Harvard started charging a modest fee for non-Harvard orders, but this did nothing to dampen the demand.

Wealth in Families turned into a publishing phenomenon because it offered something people wanted and needed, that is, advice on how to think about their family relationships and wealth, their children and philanthropy. Where others advised on the "how" of creating a legacy, Charlie explored the "why."

Moreover, Charlie tackled a key question many parents face: How do I leave my children enough money to support them on their chosen life path without thwarting their ambition to succeed on their own?

Wealth in Families has now enjoyed 11 printings, and thousands of copies are circulating among those seeking answers to the challenging questions Charlie Collier raises. After five years of unanticipated success for the book, Charlie undertook a major revision. The 2006 version of *Wealth in Families* included an introductory chapter, an updated questionnaire to evaluate your family wealth, and a new chapter on family meetings.

My wife, Maisie, and I have met with Charlie and included him in a family meeting. His ideas have proven to have great practical value for us.

Wealth in Families grows out of Charlie's personal observations and his continuing curiosity about topics ranging from family systems theory to strategic philanthropy. Yet these understandings flow from the Harvard community, where Charlie worked as the University's senior philanthropic adviser. Much of the book builds on his conversations with Harvard alumni and their advisers. While *Wealth* does not represent an "official" Harvard view of philanthropy, it does reflect the University's sustained interest in fostering philanthropy, a field that has grown dramatically in recent years.

Harvard has, for example, established the Hauser Center for Nonprofit Organizations (located at the Harvard Kennedy School) and the Whitehead Fund for Not-for-Profit Management, which supports the Business School's Initiative on Social Enterprise. These and other programs are illuminating principles and research on strategic philanthropy, social entrepreneurship, and nongovernmental organizations (NGOs) in fresh ways.

I am happy, then, that Charlie's work is evolving and remains available, especially since it can now reach a much broader audience of Harvard's alumni, their families, their advisers, and the public. I believe it will continue to be beneficial to everyone who reads it.

JAMES R. HOUGHTON

Preface

My purpose in writing *Wealth in Families* is to encourage you to think deeply about the fundamental questions surrounding your financial wealth and its effect on your family. If I am successful, you may find yourself choosing to alter the ways in which you plan and act with regard to both your wealth and your family.

After 35 years of working with individuals and families, I have discovered that the hardest, yet most rewarding, part of the planning process is asking essential questions about what is important to people—besides financial wealth—and how they can enhance each family member's growth.

These hard questions surrounding family and the wise use of money across the generations are the most important ones, and yet they are rarely asked. The questions about the meaning and purpose of wealth should drive the thinking of individuals and families, and the resulting estate planning decisions and outcomes. Think about values first, products second. This book explores three important family themes (Chapter 1), essential questions about wealth (Chapter 2), the meaning of wealth (Chapter 3), the amount of an appropriate inheritance (Chapter 4), family governance (Chapter 5), the development of a balanced approach to money (Chapter 6), financial education (Chapter 7), the philanthropic impulse (Chapter 8), and family meetings (Chapter 9). Several chapters include interviews with leading experts in the field of wealth management.

Together, these pages serve as a reflection on the meaning and purpose of family wealth. These essential "why" questions form the subtext of each chapter. I do not delve into the specific arrangements and products associated with estate planning and charitable giving because they are simply *secondary* to the questions of meaning, legacy, and how we grow great human beings.

As I began working with couples and families, I was led to the need for a book like *Wealth in Families* that addresses the deeper issues surrounding wealth. Exploring the complex landscape of family wealth has transformed my approach to my career and personal life. I have embraced the approach described in the book, introducing my sons to the joys of charitable giving, inaugurating a program of financial education, and facilitating family meetings for three generations of Colliers.

Conducting research and doing interviews for this book have also reinforced my conviction that discovering your calling and personal fulfillment truly eclipses money in importance. It is necessary to tell oneself and one's family this basic truth because it is all too easy to believe we are *defined* by what we own. Having substantial financial resources challenges us to reevaluate what really matters.

At Harvard University, it is clear that what really matters are the numerous individual gestures of care for people and programs on a human scale. Many thoughtful gifts are viewed as "investments" that can, over time, help cure disease, improve inner city schools, affect public policy, or train the next generation of leaders who will solve our social problems, to list just a few examples. Strategic philanthropy at Harvard and elsewhere can—and does—transform innumerable lives for the better.

This book is drawn from my career of service to secondary and higher education—more than half of it at Harvard. Against this backdrop, there are two important influences. The first is Phillips Academy, Andover, because it was Andover's deep commitment to service that set me on a trajectory that included summers of community service through the Quebec Labrador Foundation, majoring in religion at Dartmouth College, and earning a degree from Harvard Divinity School. Second, the strongest influence on my life has been the quiet yet profound example of my parents. They believed and communicated that there was something worth doing beyond our family. This principle of "giving back" has had a powerful and sustained effect on who I am and how I approach my work with families.

Helping alumni, their spouses, and families explore the relationship issues surrounding financial wealth, shape their philanthropy, and make tax-wise gift decisions is deeply satisfying. While the book has been written primarily for people with substantial financial wealth, its principles are universal and can be applied by almost anyone. I know that charitable giving can indeed make a difference in the lives of both donor and recipient. I hope that the questions and voices that follow can make a difference in your life, the lives of your family members, and the institutions and causes you are most passionate about.

CHARLES W. COLLIER
April 2012

ACKNOWLEDGMENTS

I am enormously grateful to a large number of friends who have inspired my passion for philanthropy. Their openness has informed the way I think about the issues surrounding money and, indeed, the true meaning and purpose of family wealth. To all of them I owe a great debt.

I wish to thank: Joanie Bronfman, Marty Carter, Terry Christensen, Paul Comstock, Ginny Esposito, Scott Fithian, Katherine Gibson, Joline Godfrey, Lee Hausner, Jay Hughes, Dennis Jaffe, Alan Jones, Peter Karoff, Kathryn McCarthy, John Messervey, Ellen Perry, Robert Putnam, Paul Schervish, Jay Steenhuysen, Kathy Wiseman, and Peter White.

I especially want to thank the alumni who gave so generously of their time, experience, and wisdom, a contribution that enriched this book: David B. Arnold, Jr. AB '44, MBA '47; Robert R. Barker AB '36; W. B. Barker AB '69, PhD '75; Edmund B. Cabot AB '65, MD '72, GSA '68; Gregory C. Carr MPP '86; Barbara and Finn M. W. Caspersen LLB '66; Jeffrey Chambers AB '76; William W. Chorske MBA '65; Abram T. Collier AB '34, LLB '37; Richard B. Covey AB '50; John A. Davis DBA '82; Charles J. Egan, Jr. AB '54; Gregory J. Englund JD '74; Michael L. Fay JD '75; Alphonse Fletcher, Jr. AB '87; Christopher F. O. Gabrieli AB '81; William W. George MBA '66; Kelin Gersick PhD '76; the Reverend Professor Peter J. Gomes BD '68; Gustave M. Hauser LLB '55; Amos B. Hostetter, Jr. MBA '61; the Reverend F. Washington Jarvis AB '61; William L. Jaques AB '69; John F. Keane, Sr. AB '53, MBA '54; William J. Kneisel MBA '74; Christine W. Letts MBA '76; Andrew K. Ludwick AB '67, MBA '69; Warren McFarlan AB '59, MBA '61, DBA '65; Andrea Okamura AB '76; Carl H. Pforzheimer III AB '58, MBA '63; David Rockefeller, Jr. AB '63; Neil L. Rudenstine PhD '64, LLD '02; Howard H. Stevenson MBA '65, DBA '69; Jennifer P. Stone AB '80, MD '86; Robert G. Stone, Jr. AB '45, LLD '03; Richard T. Watson AB '54, JD '60; William Weil AB '89, MBA '95; John C. Whitehead MBA '47, LLD '95; and William D. Zabel JD '61.

I also want to single out several colleagues whose vision, encouragement, and expertise have made a significant difference to me personally and to this project: Bill Boardman, Mary McCulloch, Geoffrey Movius, Tom Reardon, Laura Smith, Andy Tiedemann, and Frank White.

Finally, I wish to thank my wife, Sally, and my sons, Whit and Ben, for their support, patience, and willingness to let me experiment with many of the ideas expressed in this book.

CHAPTER 1

Family Anchors

Family is important.

Most people would agree with that statement because family relationships influence our life course. Someone once said that "the quality of a life is determined by the quality of one's relationships." I would add "one's *family* relationships." Many factors affect family relationships and money is key among them, both when it is abundant and when it is scarce. Yet money, and its impact on families, often pose a huge problem for those relationships: Who gets the money? Who receives the information about the family's wealth? What should be the final estate allocation? However, discussions about money can also provide an opportunity for parents and adult children to clarify their thinking about the purposes of the family's financial wealth. A family can use these conversations as an opportunity to work together and have an open discussion about an often difficult subject. Rather than divide the family, a conversation about the money, and its uses, can have a surprisingly beneficial effect on family relationships.

In fact, the most critical challenges families face are rarely financial. They are relationship-based and family-based. Asking yourself and your children essential questions can offer a resilient response to some of these challenges. My goal throughout this book is to pose questions that broaden your thinking and enable you to answer these hard questions for yourself.

What follows are some probing questions about family money and family philanthropy. There are no single or right answers. Asking the question and hearing how other family members respond are more important than the answers.

- What challenges do we face regarding our family and our money?

- What is our vision for our family's future?

- What is our family's definition of success?

- What is an appropriate financial inheritance for our children?

- What principles will guide our decisions about estate allocations?

- What has been our experience of working together as a family?

- How do we prepare our children to steward a financial inheritance?

- Should we bring our son-in-law or daughter-in-law into financial and philanthropic conversations?

- What are our core philanthropic interests and how did these come to be important to us?

- How may we enable the next generation to create a shared dream with a family foundation while also fulfilling the founder's mission?

- How do we promote a sense of togetherness in our family while also encouraging each person's individuality?

After working with many couples and families, I would suggest three organizing principles that are essential to creating effective families. First, creating and telling family stories give meaning to the experience of the family. We live our lives within the context of stories and understand reality through our self-narratives and family myths. Stories shape our lives and our relationships. So I ask families to tell their most important stories. I invite them to talk about the events we explore while looking at a diagram of their multigenerational family. We are all *meaning-makers*, and we yearn to craft a coherent account of our personal and family experience. To which stories do you return time and again to make sense of your life? What stories do justice to the facts of your family's history?

Family stories serve many purposes: to gain a sense of the family's uniqueness, to connect with the source of the family's financial wealth, and to deal with losses and transitions. Stories can also be a way by which a family begins to integrate new members. Monica McGoldrick writes about the priority of family stories in her book, *You Can Go Home Again: Reconnecting with Your Family*.

> We are born not just into our family, but into our family's stories, which both nourish and sometimes cripple us. And when we die, the stories of our lives become part of our family's web of meaning. Family stories tend to be told to remind members of the family's cherished beliefs. We sing of the heroes and even the villains whose daring the family admires. Taping or writing down the stories of older family

members can bring a richness to our search for perspective on family that cannot be achieved in any other way.

In recent years, I interviewed my father to learn the facts of my family and hear the seminal stories. I asked him penetrating questions drawn from *The Intimacy Paradox* by Donald S. Williamson. For example: Tell me about your parents' marriage? What kind of man was your father? What nurtured your own marriage over the years? Can you tell a story of when you were resilient in response to a major life challenge?

These conversations have yielded significant benefits for my family and me personally. I have discovered new facts and stories that I can pass on to my sons, my sisters, and the next generation. Understanding the emotional history of my forebears has also given me insights about my own relationships with family, work, and social life. Hearing family stories from my father has helped me to appreciate my background and to see how I am different from him and other family members. These insights allow me to make more conscious choices concerning who I want to be.

The second principle emerges from my observation that there is a tension between being an individual in a family and being a part of the whole. All families exhibit two strong emotional forces: one pushes us toward togetherness, while the other pulls us toward individuality. These counterbalancing life forces shape the way we live in ways that often are not obvious.

This tension and the amount of life energy we invest in responding to it ebb and flow over time. The equilibrium of togetherness and individuality changes automatically and deliberately over time. Some families lean more toward togetherness and others tend toward individuality. In her book, *Extraordinary Relationships*, Roberta M. Gilbert, M.D. says that when family members experience anxious times it is not uncommon to see a drive toward togetherness.

Family philanthropy can function as an activity promoting genuine family togetherness. The next generation may, however, also experience it as a pressure to conform. How then can a family negotiate a succession plan that respects the wishes of the foundation's original donor while striving to enhance the individuality of the next generation?

In many families, it is often hard for individual members to make life choices (spouse, career, religion, and lifestyle, to name a few) that are different from those that the rest of the family might make and still feel included in the larger family unit.

The third principle concerns the role parents have in encouraging their children to lead their own lives while staying connected to the family. How can you help your children leave home completely in a psychological sense while staying emotionally connected to the family? Williamson writes about how our children separate and how it can affect the ways in which they handle life's challenges, opportunities, and intimate relationships:

> How does one embrace and cherish family heritage and simultaneously transcend family emotionality? How does one create a unique self in a new generation and simultaneously belong to the old? How does one decide to make no further mortgage payments to the past and simultaneously continue to show gratitude for what has been given? How does one enjoy a strong sense of identification with one's own flesh and blood and simultaneously acquire a clear and unencumbered title to one's own life and destiny?

Encouraging our children to lead their own lives suggests a fundamental goal of parenting: to raise children who are separate *and* connected. A family should embrace the idea of rearing autonomous children. Is it possible to treat your adult children, beginning, say, at age 25, as "peers?" Such a relationship may be hard to establish, but a goal to strive for over a lifetime.

For me, the principle that undergirds this very large question of autonomy and connection is to give children permission to be different and help them to discover their true calling. This is the "passion question." How can we assist them, and perhaps other family members, to find a driving passion that they turn into meaningful work? After all, isn't this what family is supposed to do? "Passion has its own purpose," writes Robert Kegan, the William and Miriam Meehan Professor of Adult Learning and Professional Development at the Harvard Graduate School of Education, in his book, *In Over Our Heads: The Mental Demands of Modern Life*. "Passion can be a bit disdainful of reasonableness and productivity. And passion is among the most sacred and fragile gifts the gods bestow on us. It is fragile before our devastating embarrassment and impatience. And it is sacred because it promises the possibility of new life."

CHAPTER 2

Family Wealth: Asking the Essential Questions

Consider these questions:

- What is really important to your family?

- What are your family's true assets?

- What should you do to guide and support the life journey of each family member over time?

- How wealthy do you want your children to be?

- Do you feel you have a responsibility to society?

These are the deeper questions families ought to ask themselves today—and on a continuing basis. I am convinced that these questions should be asked and answered before estate planning is even discussed. You might also ask other questions, such as: What kind of family do you want to be? What do you want to accomplish—or help others to accomplish? What legacy do you want to leave your children and society? Deciding where to go with your financial success and why you want to meet those goals are the strategic questions that you should ask first. Determining how to get there and which legal arrangements to use are secondary tactical decisions.

Let your shared core values and guiding principles inform your choices. Your financial wealth is a wonderful vehicle to help you and your family members follow their passions and achieve a collective goal. In my experience, families who go through this process achieve significantly better results—financially and emotionally.

I define a successful family as one that knows who it is, what it stands for, and where it is going. Successful families manage themselves deliberately. There is much at stake for your individual family members, for your family as a whole, and for society at large. If you and your family can define "what's important" before deciding "what to do," then your children will thrive, your family will flourish, and society will benefit.

Staggering amounts of financial wealth have been produced in America since World War II, and especially in the last two decades. The result is vast personal opportunity, huge inheritances, stunning philanthropy, and a crisis of meaning. The wealthy are, in many cases, searching for a dimension beyond wealth. Increasingly, they are asking themselves penetrating questions about the purpose of financial wealth. How much is enough? How do I make sure my financial wealth creates independence rather than dependency? Can I use my wealth to make a difference to society?

These broader questions are important because the arena of values and principles, communication and trust, calling and education is critical to your children's pursuit of happiness and to the positive preservation of your family. The focus of financial wealth preservation, it turns out, is not really financial.

While tax reduction, estate planning, and legal structures are important, they alone cannot enhance your children's or your family's financial wealth over the long haul. Often, estate and tax-planning vehicles take on a life of their own. Indeed, empirical studies of successful family businesses worldwide reveal that transferring the financial aspect of the wealth to succeeding generations is often the easiest part of the preservation and succession process.

In fact, a number of well-off families pay little estate tax. "How can that be?" you may ask. The answer is that they plan ahead, defining an appropriate inheritance for their children and grandchildren. They use sophisticated techniques to transfer their financial wealth early, thereby maximizing the growth of assets in succeeding generations. Finally, they typically leave the residual of their estates to their private family foundation, various charities, or both. All of these techniques may be effectively employed, however, without resolving the crisis of meaning that substantial wealth so often engenders. Dollars are transferred, but satisfaction is not.

How, then, should you think about the deeper issues around wealth? Begin by asking your family four simple questions drawn from a business model for strategic planning taught at Harvard Business School:

1. What is your family's vision for its future?

2. Can your family members work together?

3. Can your family make joint decisions around money, philanthropy, and legacy?

4. How should your family make decisions together?

For me, these are essential questions family members must address if they are going to come to grips with the meaning of their wealth and complete a succession process effectively.

Succession planning is not just a single event symbolized by signing thoughtfully designed estate planning documents. It is an evolving, lifelong process. Preserving your financial wealth and enhancing the lives of your family members over time constitute a journey. To undertake effective succession planning, you may want to define a family vision and mission, create a structure for decision making appropriate to your family, foster open communication, and encourage the growth and development of all your family members.

"What drives all successions is a vision of the future, hammered out over time, that embraces the aspirations of both the senior and junior generations as well as those of their forebears," writes Ivan Lansberg, a family business consultant in Connecticut. In his book, *Succeeding Generations*, he says, "This vision—which I call a Shared Dream—generates the excitement and energy that every family must have to do the hard work of succession planning."

The key questions running through *Wealth in Families* are "What's important?" and "What's the effect of a given decision on your heirs?" They should be discussed before you ask yourself, "How do we get there?" I am convinced that these questions can be useful to any family, regardless of their net worth. Let me summarize my principal themes:

The meaning you give to your financial wealth is a statement of who you are

Your approach to wealth is a statement to your family of what you stand for. You and your family do stand for something, even if it is never articulated. What core values and principles does your family agree on—for example, achievement, knowledge, diversity, hard work, generosity, creativity, compassion, spirituality, justice, integrity, honesty, service, respect, or love?

Another key question focuses on the meaning and purpose of your family's financial wealth? Is its highest and best use to spend it, to provide a higher standard of living for family members, to enable family members to choose careers based on factors other than economics, to fund new family businesses, to provide a comfortable retirement, to provide for family emergencies, to provide resources for philanthropy, or a combination of all these?

Some families are quite specific about their family culture as it relates to wealth. The Rockefellers, for example, are explicit that their financial wealth is now devoted to preservation and philanthropy. On the other hand, for certain families in America, the main purpose of financial wealth is to enhance the family's ability to achieve in the political domain.

Family fortunes can, however, have corrosive effects. We continually hear about intergenerational conflict or sibling rivalry around money issues that often divides or destroys families. Money is a potent force for good or ill. It can either promote or impair initiative. We all know families for whom financial wealth has provided significant benefits: freedom, independence, access, flexibility, and enormous capacity for personal and public generosity. We also know of situations in which that same level of success contributes to curtailing personal achievement and retarding maturity. The side effects can be toxic, often creating dependency and a lack of competence.

Money casts a spell—and it can be for good. It is important, indeed critical, for families to think seriously about the meaning of their financial wealth, the messages they send to their children about money, and the example they set by their own uses of their resources. My experience is that the meaning given to money (and the family's guiding principles, for that matter) is rarely stated explicitly. Financial wealth should, perhaps, be seen as an important tool to enhance the life journey of each family member. Money can express your core values and expand your family members' pursuit of their life calling. A discussion that articulates your family's values and vision, while respecting individual differences, can strengthen your family.

There are four major kinds of family wealth: human, intellectual, social, and financial

There is more to family wealth than the financial dimension. *Human capital* refers to who individual family members are, and what they are called to do; *intellectual capital* refers to how family members learn and govern themselves; *social capital* denotes how family members engage with society at large; and *financial capital* stands for the property of the family.

Families that enhance human, intellectual, and social capital have a better chance at growing great human beings, and continuing as a cohesive group that enjoys meeting, working, and being together for more than one generation.

"Most families are only aware that they have one form of capital: financial capital," says James E. (Jay) Hughes, Jr., an estate planning lawyer and family governance specialist in New York, author of *Family Wealth: Keeping It in the Family*. Hughes is a proponent of the four forms of family wealth: "A family must know whether all of its forms of capital are growing. Rarely in my experience do families measure their human, intellectual, and social capital. Frequently, members do not even recognize that they own these forms of capital."

I believe that this broader definition of family wealth is accurate and provides a new approach to thinking about what you should actually do with your financial capital. For example, philanthropy can be a key component of a family's social capital and can provide multiple benefits to family members as well as to society. Family philanthropy is a powerful teaching tool that provides a safe environment in which your children can learn about money management and working as part of a team. Moreover, many families want to leave a legacy of *meaning* in addition to their financial wealth. Philanthropy can function as an important vehicle for articulating core values, providing a meaningful family legacy, and giving your children (and grandchildren) a competency experience. A strategic philanthropy program for family members enhances their human, intellectual, and social capital.

Successful families share effective practices in common

Successful families make thoughtful choices around their wealth and think about the effect of their decisions on the lives of their children and their spouses, and their grandchildren. Most importantly, they talk openly with their children, at age-appropriate times, about all the issues surrounding the four components of the family's true wealth.

In my experience, the best practices of successful families include the following:

1. They focus on the human, intellectual, and social capital of their family.

2. They stress the priority of each family member's individual pursuit of happiness.

3. They work on enhancing intrafamily communication.

4. Their time frame for determining success is long-term.

5. They tell and retell the family's most important stories.

6. They create mentor-like relationships when establishing family trusts.

7. They have collaboratively defined a family vision statement (the Shared Dream).

8. They teach children and grandchildren the competencies and responsibilities that come with financial wealth.

9. They work at getting to really know each family member.

10. They give their younger family members as much responsibility as they can manage as soon as possible.

Of course, no family achieves all of these objectives, but attempting to do so is a goal to which any family can aspire over a lifetime.

––––––––––

When I ask parents what their deepest hopes are for their children, they often say they just want them to be happy. But how should we think about happiness? Is it simply a pleasant emotion or something more? According to Aristotle and his latter-day student, Thomas Jefferson, the "pursuit of happiness" has to do with an internal journey to know ourselves and an external journey of selfless service to others. Indeed, the concept of a personal moral compass has been a central motif throughout the lifetime of our civilization.

More recently, Abraham Maslow, the twentieth-century American psychologist, gave us clues to real happiness in his hierarchy of human needs and goals. Self-actualization, the final aspiration, involves the journey through which we discover what we are truly called to do and be and starting to do it. Maslow postulated an additional objective: transcendence, the ability to move beyond the "self," to see one's own fulfillment as inextricably linked to serving the needs of others.

The Rev. F. Washington Jarvis, headmaster emeritus of the Roxbury Latin School, says that true happiness in life comes from a long-term vision of our life. Jarvis writes in his book, *With Love and Prayers*, "Important, though, as a vision is [regarding career and lifestyle], it is nothing like as important as an overall vision for your whole life. We might call such a vision existential; it has to do with the discovery by you of some meaning and purpose to your whole existence. Inevitably such a vision must entail not only finding meaning in your life but meaning also in your inevitable death." He goes on to say, "If you want to be happy, you must learn to love: to pay the price of caring for others, of putting them first, of inconveniencing yourself. That is the pathway to happiness."

Enhancing your individual family members' pursuits of happiness so that they thrive over time is a worthwhile journey. Indeed, it may be the most important journey you will undertake. I suggest that you focus on each family member's discovery and fulfillment of his or her life calling by dedicating your family's human, intellectual, social, and financial capital to that higher purpose. In the end, what we really care about is much deeper than financial wealth. The desire for meaning and genuine connection will always transcend wealth. As my father wrote years ago, "To be really rich is to be rich in achievement, rich in experience, and rich in friendship."

CHAPTER 3

Exploring the Meaning of Wealth

"No, next Tuesday is out. Friday is no good. How about never? Is never good for you?" These are the words of the busy executive pictured in a *New Yorker* cartoon, consulting his calendar as he talks on the phone at his desk. Many wealthy individuals are indeed so busy with their businesses and lives that they rarely take the time to think about the bigger issues surrounding their family's wealth. It's my experience, however, that a growing number of wealthy individuals are extremely interested in the deeper issues around money and its impact on their families. Busy though they are, these people are making the time to talk about their concerns.

Paul G. Schervish, professor of sociology and director of the Social Research Institute at Boston College, agrees. He has spent part of his academic life interviewing wealthy individuals to understand their biographical narratives. He believes that a distinctive characteristic of the wealthy is the significance of the path they often take to use their resources to care for others, "to provoke questions about the quality of wants" and "to awaken sensibilities of gratitude." Their wealth, he suggests, has the potential to deepen their sense of themselves.

"I argue that religion or spirituality encourages philanthropy by explicitly linking givers to the concerns and needs of others," says Schervish in his essay, "Wealth and the Spiritual Secret of Money." "My analysis follows a three-step logic: (1) if *wealth* affords individuals the ability to have what they want (at least in the material realm), and (2) if *philanthropy* can be understood as the transformation of time and money from a pool of wealth into a disposable gift to others, (3) *religion*—as it takes form in what I call the spirituality of money—motivates or spurs philanthropy, in amount and type, by shaping the quality of wants or desires among the wealthy. If the wealthy generally can have what they want, it is the realm of spirituality that directs their wants into a bond of care for others."

Substantial financial wealth, whether created or inherited, has the capacity to transform the wealth holder. Many wealthy individuals rethink the meaning of their money, indeed their lives, in light of the freedom and empowerment their money provides them. I see it in investment bankers and inheritors in their forties, who take time off to assess what they might do next with their lives. Some return to undertake a new business venture, while others become serious philanthropists; still others decide to study music or teach high school. I have watched money managers and company presidents in their fifties and sixties make dramatic changes in their lives and devote significant time and financial resources to charitable purposes. Here are three examples:

- **Andrew K. Ludwick.** Andy is an entrepreneur. He cofounded SynOptics Communications (which became Bay Networks, Inc., a successful Silicon Valley computer company) and was its CEO until 1997. At that time, age 51, he faced a transition:

  "I took some time off because I wasn't sure what I wanted to do. I didn't want to start or run another company, since I had just done that for forty-eight quarters. I wanted to explore other things and welcomed this midlife opportunity.

  "I settled on being an investor and board member for a number of Internet startups in the Valley as a way to contribute to the field I know something about. I am also pursuing other interests: more personal time with my wife and children, new involvements in the local community, and a serious focus on philanthropy. Harvard was a catalyst and started me on the philanthropic track. My initial gift of networking equipment from SynOptics had a profound impact on Harvard and taught me that I could make a difference through giving.

  "There was a fork in the road, and I redefined how I would spend my time and energy in many dimensions. Money gave me a set of choices, free time, and the wherewithal to build enterprises in a field that will change the world."

- **Christopher F. O. Gabrieli.** While on leave from medical school in the 1980s, Chris founded a health-care software company that was backed by Bessemer Ventures, a Boston venture capital company. He never returned to his studies. "I was persuaded by Bill Burgin to join the firm and concentrate on health care investing full time," he says, explaining his first career as a venture capitalist. "I liked the partners and was excited to support new ideas that turn into useful companies."

  Chris took six months off in 1998 to run for the U.S. Congress in the Democratic primary in Massachusetts. Although he lost, the experience proved to be a turning point and launched him into a second career, including running for governor in 2006:

"What began as a deep interest in public policy was becoming a bigger part of my life. I have a new career and am now involved in a number of Boston civic organizations—for example, MassINC, a leading think tank on pragmatic policy and economic planning, and the Boston Plan for Excellence, whose mission is to help reorganize Boston public schools.

"Reflecting on my past, I also realize the degree to which the generosity and foresight of others allowed me to succeed in life. I am clearly fortunate with my financial success and feel a responsibility to further the great institutions in Boston and help create new ones. For example, I think I bring something to the two committees I serve on at the Harvard School of Public Health because of my background in health-care investing and policy. It's interesting, fun, and intellectually stimulating to help them meet and solve real social problems.

"My resources allowed me to dig into a second career in public policy and retool myself to acquire the skills and knowledge to make a new contribution. I had the chance at thirty-eight, rather than fifty-eight, to start another career. My money gave me the freedom to pursue my passion for public policy and philanthropy."

- **William J. Kneisel.** After many years as an investment banker at Morgan Stanley in New York, Bill took a six-month sabbatical in 1996 to reassess his objectives:

"After years of public offerings and mergers, I discovered it wasn't as rewarding any more. The values had changed, and there was more focus on money and transactions for their own sake rather than the earlier goals of solving client problems. The client focus that I learned from my mentors in the business, Fred Whittemore and Tom Saunders, was a kind of 'sacred trust.' I had come to the point in my life where I was calling into question what I was doing. The sabbatical gave me the time and space to reflect on where I was going.

"I thought of teaching at a business school, briefly tried working for a smaller firm, and eventually retired. I am going in a different direction now, spending more time with my family, rereading the classics, undertaking a few projects for Morgan Stanley, and enjoying lots of volunteer and charitable work for schools I care about, such as the Hopkins School and Middlebury College. My new life is still evolving, but my financial wherewithal has clearly allowed me to reorder my priorities and think through questions of meaning."

What we see unfolding is the archetype of the hero's journey: the "call," the departure, and the return. In the lives of the wealthy, it is an existential shift, often more of an inner journey than outward accomplishment. They are navigating a response to a change in their lives, frequently driven by the presence of new wealth. Consciously, they take a leave of absence to explore their options, and in this transitional work they go through a stage of development in regard to their finances.

"Our research," says Schervish, in his introduction to the book *Gospels of Wealth*, "reveals that for many respondents, both those who earned and those who inherited their wealth—a major transformation in consciousness takes place at some point with regard to that wealth. This point may arrive quietly and gradually or appear as a dramatic realization."

Schervish uses the concept of "liminality" to explain the personal evolution of wealth holders. "Liminality denotes the boundaries between and passage through different stages of life and identity that occur at important turning points, such as becoming an entrepreneur or receiving the first installment of a substantial inheritance. By focusing on these periods of liminality, respondents highlight the intricate process of change by which they move from one stage of their relation to money to the next and hence from one stage of their identity to another."

In his book, *Succeeding Generations*, Ivan Lansberg echoes the concept of liminality with his exploration of the role of a Shared Dream in the lives of families with financial fortunes or private businesses. He makes the case that a Shared Dream, or vision of the future, is critical to the effective succession of families and family businesses. He draws on the work of Daniel Levinson, the late Yale professor of psychology, who wrote *The Seasons of a Man's Life*, to stress how the Dream can give meaning to one's life and is tied to various stages of life in developmental psychology.

"Levinson believed that the Dream is reworked during certain key transitional periods in the life cycle," Lansberg writes. "This is part of an intermittent process that combines periods of stability, in which the key elements do not change, with transitional periods, in which certain aspects of the Dream may be altered to bring them more in line with reality and the individual's internal needs."

One of the most common results of these individual transformations around family wealth is a new or renewed commitment to philanthropy. Paul Schervish heard about this phenomenon repeatedly during his interviews:

> The wealthy move beyond pursuing private interest as their public contribution to pursuing public needs as their personal concern. Those who do so may be described as having learned the spiritual secret of money. The scope of their self-interest increasingly broadens and deepens to include a greater diversity of people and needs.

Financial wealth is a tool to achieve greater ends, for individuals and for society. Thus, philanthropy has a dual purpose. First, it is a vehicle for expressing core values—for individuals and for families. Typically, these values might include educational opportunity, advancement of knowledge, artistic freedom, alleviation of suffering, eradication of disease, or environmental preservation.

Second, philanthropy is the tangible expression of care for others outside one's immediate family. Schervish defines philanthropy as the social relation of care in which individuals expand the horizons of their self-interest to include meeting the needs of others. "It is the virtue of *care*," writes Schervish in an introductory essay for his book, *Care and Community in Modern Society*:

> The term care derives, of course, from the Latin *caritas*. The philanthropist is first and foremost a caregiver, not a giver of time and money. Time and money are the medium by which care is expressed. But the fundamental moral standard to which philanthropists should dedicate themselves is caring for others in need.

> Caring individuals come to view themselves and others in a different light. To exhibit a caring orientation toward others in a constant and dedicated fashion is to assume a self-definition in which one does not so much become selfless as self-expansive. A caring person is one who becomes profoundly self-concerned about what happens to others by identifying with their fate.

To explore the deeper meaning and purpose of family wealth, I interviewed Paul Schervish in his Chestnut Hill office. What follows is an edited version of an extensive interview.

COLLIER: In your experience, what do people consider to be the "meaning" of wealth?

SCHERVISH: The meaning of wealth is fundamentally freedom. It's freedom from material constraints and the constraints of time. It's a dialectic between freedom from and freedom to. The freedom to, on the material side, is to be able to purchase what you want, to go where you want, to have what you want in the material realm.

Freedom in the temporal realm is often a way of retrieving the past. When things go wrong and you have wealth, you can often correct a mistake or a problem. You can shape to some extent the present and the future.

Emotionally, wealth is freedom too. There's a psychological empowerment, a mixture of confidence that you can have what you want and you have the ability to carry it out. On a psychological level, it enables you to have both great expectations, and the confidence to achieve them.

You may remember that at the very beginning of Charles Dickens's *David Copperfield*, David says he does not know "whether I shall turn out to be the hero of my own life." Most wealth holders wonder the same thing in their contemplative moments. But, for the most part, they can eventually, at least in the material realm, answer that, yes, they are the heroes of their own lives. And they not only shape their own lives but also the lives of others.

COLLIER: Don't wealthy individuals often struggle with the "meaning" question at some point?

SCHERVISH: Yes, they do. But, for me, this question brings up the larger issue of the effect of wealth on spirituality.

The question is this: Does wealth enable you to be more or less spiritual? Doesn't financial wealth undercut your spirituality? Or perhaps we should ask: Is the terrain of virtue and vice different for different groups of income and wealth?

These questions are becoming more important because a larger and larger number of people have more and more wealth, which not only makes the question individual but cultural. It forces one to ask, "If you can have what you want in the material realm, what is it that you want in the spiritual realm?"

I think the terrain of spirituality—of virtue and vice—is different for wealth holders. The dialectics of care and control are different. But remember, wealth is like fire. It can enchant and deepen some, but it can burn and destroy others.

COLLIER: You have discussed the concept of "liminality" in your writing. Can you explain that term?

SCHERVISH: What I mean by liminality is those special periods that are identifiable as psychological turning points in our lives, where we reach a crossroads or a threshold. When we leave one part of our life and enter another, it speaks of a personal transformation; a kind of life, death, and rebirth. At such times what happens in terms of financial wealth is a death of an old way of thinking, feeling, and acting around the money and a rebirth of a new way.

COLLIER: Can you give an example?

SCHERVISH: Yes, I talked the other day with a man who said, "Now that I am wealthy, having liquidated my business, I'm going to take a trip to Europe to consider what I am going to do next."

COLLIER: Is this a form of the ancient myth of the hero's journey?

SCHERVISH: Yes, it's an awakening, a vision quest. A lot of these things are happening simultaneously. It's a search for his identity. It's a search for what he's going to do with his time. It's a search for what he's going to do with his money. Not that this is a terrible fate, but on some emotional level he felt something old was passing and something new was in the offing. And he didn't quite know what it was.

Such an experience often occurs when wealth holders sell a business or receive a financial windfall, when their children grow up and move away, or when they retire. What happens in every point of liminality is that there's a transition. It doesn't mean the person becomes more or less virtuous. All it means is that they are struggling with the change of the terrain of their spiritual life. They hope that the next stage will be deeper.

When an individual has $20 million, for example, there's a liminality in which the children are seen as being part of the transformation. He may say, "I am now at the end of my time as an accumulator of wealth, and in this new period I am passing this on to my children." There is an initiation rite that goes on for the children as well as for the wealth holder. Passing the baton is a period of liminality.

COLLIER: Many parents struggle with the question of passing on a financial inheritance. What kind of legacy do they want to leave their children with respect to their values?

SCHERVISH: There's a spiritual legacy and there's a material legacy. Legacy is exactly what is being looked at during these points of liminality. "Where have I come from? Who am I now? How do I want to shape my future? What do I want for my children?"

Legacy and liminality are really quite intertwined. They can be handled explicitly, or [they can be] ignored and happen by default. Whether you like it or not, you're going to go through liminality. You're going to leave a legacy whether you plan to or not. If we are wise, we recognize the periods of liminality, ritualize them, and celebrate them.

COLLIER: You've spoken of passing financial wealth to children and to charity. How do you decide on the right balance?

SCHERVISH: That's a good question, and it already has the answer in it. The question is, How do you do the archaeology around the connection of your financial wealth to your identity and your legacy to your family? Considering death is the classic occasion for exploring the meaning of life. We hope that the prospect of death turns out to be a positive motivator to go through the liminal period explicitly and productively, asking questions like "What do I stand for? Do I have a responsibility beyond my family?"

I believe an answer is to create significance in the light of our death, and one powerful way to accomplish this is through personal and family philanthropy. Philanthropy is financial care, but charitable giving is not the only outcome. It's financial care in many different ways. Some people transfer their business to their workers or give bonuses to the people who made them wealthy. That is as much financial care as contributing money to an inner-city school.

A lot of entrepreneurs will say that the most important way in which they're caring in the material realm is to build a business, to create jobs, and to make other people independent. The variable in all of this is not how much you give via philanthropy but how much *care* you are giving.

COLLIER: You have said the philanthropy of the wealthy creates their moral identity, linking their destiny with the destiny of others. Can you explain?

SCHERVISH: I believe what motivates care is identification. In the identification model, the giver identifies with the recipient. Where am I most deeply developed, experienced, and expressed in regard to others? In formulating the great Aristotelian and Judeo-Christian traditions, Thomas Aquinas insisted that the issue isn't the lack of self. It's the unity of love of self, love of God, and love of neighbor. What we're seeing is the way in which wealth holders care for others as if those were often themselves—or their children.

Why is it that wealth holders give so much to educational institutions, especially those with which they are associated? Similarly, why is it that the religious organizations and churches receive so much of the giving in America? It's because this kind of charitable giving is based on their identification with others. To the extent we are looking at hungry children, or people in need of education, at a deeper level we are looking at ourselves. Identification generates generosity.

COLLIER: How important is it for wealth holders to transfer to their children a legacy of care for others?

SCHERVISH: They are going to transfer legacies of meaning as well as financial wealth, whether they think about it or not. What people ought to do is to reflect on the activity so as to do it in a better way. There are people who can't or won't do this. My parents communicated a legacy of financial care as well as religious meaning to me without going into it explicitly.

Today, wealth holders with such large estates are beginning to plan their wills explicitly, think about their estates explicitly, and strategize about how to give their money away intelligently. They are now paying attention to the way in which they want their kids to think about a financial inheritance.

The questions around financial wealth are increasingly put on the table. The issue is not so much whether it's going to be done well or done poorly but whether it is to be done all at once or gradually. Financial education is best done over time.

Nothing is irretrievable. People will say, "Well, I messed this up from the time my kids were small." Well, all that does is leave an opportunity to work anew on a deeply meaningful legacy.

COLLIER: Is there a role for family philanthropy?

SCHERVISH: Yes, you want to pass on a legacy of financial care. In some instances, it may mean a very formal and structured approach with a family foundation and a mission statement.

In other cases, you may want a strategy that allows your children to decide for themselves what to do with the inheritance, saying, "You could use this money for your own personal consumption, or you could give some of it away to improve society."

If your children make the decisions themselves, you may have given them a far better legacy. Children who make that decision have an important experience: the same decision that you once had to make yourself.

· This gets to a deeper question. Does money corrupt, or [does it] open opportunity? We know the answer. It can do both. The very dynamic that we go through ourselves, wanting to make our own decisions, can provide a meaningful legacy.

We should instill a learning process by which children are always trying to figure out for themselves, with their own children and spouses, what it is that produces happiness.

COLLIER: How do the wealthy help their children to make good decisions around financial wealth?

SCHERVISH: First of all, recognize that grown children are going to make their own decisions anyway. The real question is:

How do wealth holders help create the circumstances for their children to make wise decisions? For example, around the family philanthropic process, you might say, "What are your passions and how do you want to support them?" You have to allow them to give to the causes they care about and in ways and amounts that they decide.

Dealing with personal property, you might say, "I hope that this summer home or that heirloom stays in our family forever." Approach it as a desire. What you want to do is to help your children learn the process of discernment.

Education regarding discernment means that parents are guides. What you're doing is helping your children make decisions about the way in which their identity and their money are going to carry out care in the world.

We want to teach them how to discern what needs to be done. Caring is helping others in their true needs. True needs for others are going to change over time. What we have to do is teach people a process of caring, through wise choices, in which they connect their material means with their spiritual intention. Again, we see that empowerment and material effectiveness are linked to meaning and happiness. It's in making this connection between the financial wealth and the meaning that we find our deeper identity.

COLLIER: What do you mean by children's "identity"?

SCHERVISH: Their moral identity or deepest sense of themselves. I believe in encouraging an attitude where money is seen as an instrument to their true happiness.

For any child and any adult, there is no perfect use of money. But there will surely be a very inadequate use of money unless the opportunity for mistakes and choices concerning money is encouraged. You might end up with your children carrying out a kind of "bronze" legacy of money—they do it your way. But if we want them to carry out a "golden" legacy with money, they're going to have to learn to discern for themselves the difference between superficial and deeper happiness.

COLLIER: How do parents "let go" and allow their children to make choices concerning inherited financial wealth?

SCHERVISH: Letting go of control is very difficult for many parents and more difficult for them to do with their money than, for example, with a decision about what college their children will attend.

I believe that wealthy parents have to think deeply about what really matters to them and about what their financial wealth means to them. If they think in these terms and express their thoughts, their children will listen to them.

"Letting go" doesn't mean that you simply leave your children as sheep without a shepherd. Your shepherding is your communication to them of the happiness that you create and experience by the wise use of your money.

CHAPTER 4

Defining a Financial Inheritance: How Much Is Enough?

"Part of the reason for believing that my wealth should be given back to society," says Bill Gates, in a *Forbes* magazine article, "and not, in any substantial percentage, be passed on to my children, is that I don't think it would be good for them. They really need to get out and work and contribute to society. I think that's an important element of a fulfilling life."

Gates has touched on the defining questions: How do we provide financial security for our children while ensuring that they achieve on their own? How do you make sure a financial inheritance will help and not hinder their life journeys?

The hardest estate planning question is how much money to give to your children. The question is not how much they *could* receive but rather how much they *should* receive. How much is right for your children, and can you quantify the amount? We want our children to benefit by our family's financial wealth, but at the same time we want them to pursue a fulfilling life. How much, then, is enough? Is more always better? What is the financial wealth meant to accomplish? What is the message to our children if the primary motivation of our estate plan is the avoidance of taxes?

"How much to pass on to your children is the basic philosophical question," says William D. Zabel, a senior partner in the New York law firm of Schulte Roth & Zabel and author of *The Rich Die Richer and You Can Too*. "How much do you want them to have is a better question than how much can we get to them. Passing on all the money sends a message that financial wealth is all-important. Answering this question also leads to how, when, and in what form."

I have talked to many thoughtful alumni and some of this country's most capable estate planning lawyers on this subject, and a variety of themes—and amounts—have emerged. The issues around financial inheritance fall into four categories: how much do you give your children; when; in what form; and how much do you tell them?

How much is an appropriate financial inheritance?

What would be best for your children? What do you hope they will accomplish with the money? Making a considered and deliberate decision is wise because, if you don't, *you've actually made a decision*. You have picked the default position; that is, all to my children, less a significant percentage to the government. Spending time on inheritance planning may allow you to transfer the amount you eventually have in mind to your children while making gifts to charity, rather than to the government through taxes. The choices are not your children or taxes, but your children and charity and *no taxes*.

You might identify how the financial inheritance is to be used by your heirs—for example, grandchildren's education, down payment on a primary residence, maintenance fund for the family summer house, medical emergency fund, business opportunity fund, or financial security fund. Assign a dollar amount to the items and funds that you value and total the amount. That could be the starting point for thinking seriously about the financial inheritance that would be best for your children or grandchildren.

One other purpose of a financial inheritance is often mentioned: the career development fund. In discussing his views on the uses of a financial inheritance, the late Robert G. Stone, Jr., chairman emeritus of the Kirby Corporation in New York and former Senior Fellow of Harvard College, said it well: "I believe in giving your children enough money so they can follow whatever pursuit they want in life. If they want to be teachers or artists, I hope they will be the best they can be in those fields. Having money gives them freedom of choice with security, no matter what direction they decide to take."

This is a compelling approach—that is, thinking about the purpose of the financial inheritance as a tool to enhance many aspects of our children's lives. "I want to have a positive impact on their lives when it matters," said the late Richard T. Watson, then senior partner in the Cleveland law firm of Spieth, Bell, McCurdy & Newell. "I want them to make wise choices around schooling, houses, and travel. I want to broaden their horizons, prepare them to manage the money, and help them enjoy a richer life.

"I think about the proper amount of an initial inheritance in terms of a base level of income ($50,000 to $100,000, for example) that will free them to pursue whatever career they decide is best for them. My goal is to enhance their quality of life. For me, getting them $1 million to $2 million in their late twenties or early thirties, ideally in a generation-skipping trust with the children as cotrustees, is an attractive plan."

If deciding on a financial inheritance were always that simple! In reality, thorny questions inevitably arise. Here are a few examples: "Since we are a blended family, how do I factor in my wife's children? How do I solve the of my younger second wife, where my children may not receive an inheritance until after *she* dies? I have been giving my older grandchildren $20,000 a year for many years. How do I make up the difference with the arrival of my newest granddaughter? Should I base my decision on the amount of the capital or the amount of income the capital will generate? My children have different needs; how do I treat everyone fairly?"

The question of fair versus equal is a difficult one. An alumnus in Boston, wrestling with his own situation, puts it this way: "How do I treat my children equally when they are not equal? They have different vocations, money styles, earning powers, and marital situations." Of course, there is no one answer because families and children do and will differ. I suggest you deal with the question directly and talk about it openly, often with your adult children. Many people will help out children during their lifetime based on need, but large inter vivos transfers and bequests of significance will tend to be equal. "You have to be flexible," adds Bill Zabel, "to take into account the differences among your children and how they change over time."

The decision on how much to give or leave your children is a deeply personal one, and there are many variables, including individual preferences and specific family situations. Having said that, and admitting there are no rules of thumb, I'll make some observations using hard numbers.

In my experience, with families where the publicly traded financial wealth is in the range of $15 million to $30 million, the opening number is typically $1 million to $2 million per child. In most cases, the amount provides a measure of flexibility, but it may not dramatically change the child's lifestyle. Also, I see many people deciding that $3 million to $5 million is an appropriate financial inheritance. For families with approximately $100 million and above, many believe that $10 million to $15 million per child is sufficient. Finally, for families with a net worth greater than $500 million, the inheritance often ranges from $25 million to $50 million or more.

In many long-term wealthy families, there often exists a network of trusts and foundations, and an expectation that the financial wealth will be passed along to succeeding generations. "These families have a culture that inculcates the sense that you are fortunate," says Michael L. Fay, senior partner of the Boston law firm of Wilmer Hale, and former vice president of The Family Firm Institute. "The money has been handed to you under certain conditions. Your obligation is to be stewards and manage your affairs to maximize the wealth and pass on the principal to the next generation."

On the other hand, entrepreneurs and other self-made wealth creators often have a different inheritance strategy for their children. Sometimes, they

as much financial wealth as possible so that their children will
ιggle as they did or to preserve a majority position in a family
ε often, however, the key concern for entrepreneurs is how to
ιdren "hungry."

preneurs enjoy the hunt," adds Fay, "and they want to instill that
sense of struggle and achievement in their children. They'll set up a safety net
for them so they can be teachers or musicians—to expand their range of fulfilling life opportunities. They'll tell their own story about how excited they are in
creating something in the hope that their children will challenge themselves."

"How much is enough?" is a difficult question, but it is important to
define and quantify an appropriate amount for each of your children. Looked
at another way, the question is: How do I prevent my children from becoming
dependent "trust funders"? Of course, this is a question requiring education,
not a financial decision.

On the other hand, "How much is enough?" can lead us to ask the following: If financial wealth provides freedom, what does it mean to be free? "At
the deepest level, the question is one of freedom," says Jay Hughes. "I believe
you need to think seriously about what this means to your family.

"True economic freedom is the ability to wake up in the morning and
be able to decide what you will do for the day," Hughes concludes. "Thus, an
appropriate inheritance may be that amount of financial wealth that will allow
you to live in this way. *Any amount of money beyond that is discretionary because
it is not what you need to be free.* More money than you need can also lead to a
shadow side to freedom—which on the one hand is dependence and on the
other is license, or freedom without self-discipline. This is the paradox of the
question of 'How much is enough?'"

When should you transfer a financial inheritance to your heirs?

To decide on the best time to make a transfer to another generation, you must
first decide on the amount of assets you will need to maintain your lifestyle
for your lifetime.

If you have more than you will need, then you may be in a position to
advance some or all of the financial inheritance you have in mind to your heirs
during your lifetime.

Lifetime transfers, even if they are subject to gift taxes, are less expen-
sive than testamentary gifts to your heirs. Although the estate and gift tax
rates are the same, the gift tax is effectively 35.5 percent—much less than an
estate tax rate that can exceed 48 percent. The reason is that the gift tax paid

is not itself subject to gift taxes, that is, it is "tax-exclusive." However, any estate tax paid is itself subject to taxes, or "tax-inclusive." For example, (under recent law) it takes only $1.55 million to give your children $1 million during your lifetime, while $2.2 million would be required to leave them $1 million through your estate.

"It makes more sense to give money to your children during your lifetime than at your death," said Dick Watson. "Leaving money to your children at your death is not nearly as tax-effective. Also, the money often arrives too late to have a positive impact on your children's lives."

Moreover, early transfers of wealth to your children and grandchildren allow the money to appreciate in the younger generation—the one with the longest time horizon. Jay Hughes suggests that the model of the "investor allocator" is a way to make sure families direct new investments with high-growth potential to the proper generation. "The 'investor allocator' chooses the family member or members to actually make the investment based on their proximity to the payment of estate taxes," says Hughes. "Normally, the oldest family member will buy the investment offering the lowest growth, and the youngest family member will buy the investment offering the highest growth."

So when would it be best for your heirs to receive their inheritance? People tend to choose one of two approaches. First, define the inheritance and give it to them sooner rather than later. Talk with them, provide age-appropriate financial education, and help them understand and work with the money. Financial education and discussion of wealth responsibility are critical to this approach. Openness and access early on, coupled with education, also enhance their ability to choose careers not solely based on the economics of the profession.

Alternatively, many individuals and advisers suggest that they want to make sure their children have the chance to "make it on their own," and thus they prefer to transfer the inheritance around age 35 or later. Moreover, I know a number of people who do not want to burden their children with the issues surrounding money management in their twenties, when they should be focused on starting a career.

For many families of wealth, the answer to the question of when to transfer the inheritance lies somewhere in the middle—that is, introducing the money (and the appropriate financial education) over time. For example, give your children their college money to manage themselves. At 21, give them enough capital so they can learn the basics of investing firsthand. Add more capital at 30, and still greater portions of the financial inheritance after 35.

All of this, of course, is subject to the maturity of your children and the confidence you have in their judgment at various stages. If you have an investment whiz who is trading securities online at 17, you may want to transfer more financial wealth earlier. On the other hand, a child who is struggling to find a "calling" in his or her late twenties may be better served by receiving a partial inheritance at age 35.

"Reasonable people can certainly differ on the question of what is the appropriate age to advance the financial inheritance," added Dick Watson. "I believe that eighteen is simply too young, and giving children $100,000 at twenty-one may be better. A large inheritance—$1 million and up—should come later. Remember, we want the money to have a positive impact and free them to make choices in their lives. Failure to get the bulk of the inheritance to them by age forty is just as wrong as giving them a lot of money at eighteen."

Sometimes you just cannot be precise. I have seen situations where the company of an alumnus is about to be sold and he transfers a large block of stock to his eight-year-old son's trust. Within months, the trust is worth $7 million, perhaps more than the parents had anticipated. Frequently, venture capitalists fund their children's trusts with their carried interest, often resulting in a huge run-up in the financial inheritance. Often, they ask, "I may have done the right thing from an estate planning point of view, but did I do the right thing by them?"

What form should the financial inheritance take?

To trust or not to trust? That continues to be a key question. Properly structured, trusts can have a variety of positive benefits, including long-term tax savings, while providing "control without ownership." Of course, there are other sophisticated discounting and valuation strategies that save transfer taxes, such as family limited partnerships, charitable lead trusts, and defective grantor trusts, to name a few. But we should also be concerned with how the financial inheritance will be held and perceived by the inheritor. What will be the messages surrounding the trust? What will be the education that comes with the trust?

"Trusts make a lot of sense when you consider the issues of creditors, divorce, taxes, and premature death," says Michael Fay. "I typically make the trusts discretionary (providing a mechanism for disbursements based on trustee discretion) to ensure that the children are fully formed, achieving adults. I also want the adult children to be cotrustees (one of three, for example) and have the power to change the individual or corporate trustees."

Moreover, the quality of the human relationship between the beneficiary and trustee may be more important than the legal arrangement, says Jay Hughes in his article, "The Trustee as Mentor." "The solution to a successful beneficiary/trustee relationship lies in the trustee offering and the beneficiary accepting the proposition that at the inception of the trust, the trustee's role is to be the beneficiary's mentor and to remain in that role until the beneficiary is fully participating in the beneficiary/trustee relationship, at which time the trustee's role will evolve to the trustee as a representative."

Trusts can be a useful substitute for or complement to a prenuptial agreement when you want to preserve the family's financial wealth. "It's far better to create a trust that will protect your children's money from a disaffected spouse," said Dick Watson, "than to require their marriage to start off with an adversarial financial discussion, often precipitated by the raising of a prenuptial agreement."

Trusts make sense, and you can design terms that provide great flexibility for a beneficiary. It is also clear that, for many families, part of the financial inheritance should not be in trust but should go outright, with no strings attached. The lives of adult children can be enhanced with access to money for cars, houses, and further schooling. Most importantly, adult children need to have the money unfettered to *learn* how to deal with it, own it, and manage it. They need the freedom to take risks, to make mistakes, and, often, to fail. One approach is to give them a modest amount of money outright at age 21 or 25, monitor their progress, and then give them the balance of the financial inheritance around 35 to 40, often in trust. In summary, I believe that where substantial money is involved, the form of the financial inheritance should be a combination of outright gifts and *very* flexible trusts.

How much do you tell them?

People are often too secretive about family wealth. The problem with the "we're not going to talk about it" mentality is that it breeds mistrust and misinformation. Often, a lot of time and energy are spent by family members trying to find out the family secrets!

Secrecy surrounding the family's financial situation often begins between spouses. Many wealth holders don't tell their spouses how much money they have or how it is invested. An open and frank discussion is essential if spouses are going to work together on inheritance planning and eventually talk with their children. Sharing financial information with your spouse makes sense because this is the person with whom you are going to discuss sharing the information with your children.

There is also the issue of financial inequality between spouses. For example, a husband creates significant wealth and his wife has nothing of her own. Does it matter? "People don't think about the question of whether a spouse without money ought to have his or her own money so they don't have to *ask* for it," said Dick Watson. "I ask wealth holders—typically husbands—if their spouse has money of their own, and the response is often, 'No, but she can have whatever she wants.' I suggest he give his wife a significant amount of money so that she doesn't have to ask. This is often a transforming experience, changing the power and trust in the relationship for the better."

More communication is almost always better. Talking to your children *early* about the meaning and purpose of your family wealth can also enhance your relationship with your children.

"Many clients don't talk to their children about their wealth," says Gregory J. Englund, a Boston attorney and author of *Beyond Death and Taxes: A Guide to Total Wealth Control*. "They're fatalistic about it and don't realize that the estate tax is a voluntary tax.

"Since the basic goal of the estate plan is often to benefit the children, why not include them in the discussion?" asks Englund. "Talk with your children about the family money—over time, in an incremental way. Ideally, I suggest you tell them together even if it's early for one child and late for another, for example, when they are ages 21 and 25. In my experience, this approach reduces the possibility of sibling friction around the information. Offer them some choice. They may say that they prefer to have part of their share of an inheritance go to grandchildren and to a family foundation. Share your vision with them.

"Turn around the government's default plan," Englund adds, "and you decide, in consultation with your children, how to organize your family's financial wealth. A wonderful part of this whole approach is that your children talk to one another. The expression of this concept will vary from family to family, but what a powerful dialogue. What an opportunity for your family!"

"We talked at length with our children about our money, beginning early in their teenage years," said the late Robert R. Barker, an investment professional in New York. "For many years, we gave each of them the maximum allowable tax-free gift—$20,000 a year—and told them that our hope was that they would accumulate this for future use. Along with their grandfather, we also gave each of them $350,000 in a generation-skipping trust. We discussed everything, including asking them, 'How much do *you* think is enough?'"

"I am now leaving the bulk of my estate to charity," added Barker. "I am fortunate that I can talk to my children about our wealth and show how the rest of my money can be productive for society."

CHAPTER 5

Family Parenting: Managing Family

The most important "assets" of your family are its individual members. A governance structure designed to enhance everyone's personal growth and development may preserve your family over the long term. Are your children thriving in their chosen calling? How do they interact within your family and with society at large? Your family will survive and thrive if each family member is pursuing his or her potential for growth and happiness.

That is the main thesis of an important book, *Family Wealth: Keeping It in the Family*, by James E. Hughes, Jr. "What each family member is called to do is the critical component in keeping the family wealthy," says Hughes. "Each human being is called to an individual life journey, and to discover one's calling is the single most important duty of each human being. A family's duty is to work to preserve the family's principal wealth-generating assets: its human and intellectual capital. The family leadership and governance structure should provide an environment that values and enhances each family member's ability to pursue their individual life calling."

As we discussed in Chapter 1, Hughes suggests that four kinds of wealth need to be preserved within families:

Human capital refers to the individual family members: their knowledge, talents, spirituality, values, passions, dreams, and aspirations. Most importantly, the term also refers to their defining who they are called to be and what they are called to do.

"Education and training are the most important investments in human capital," writes Gary S. Becker, professor of economics and sociology at the University of Chicago and a winner of the Nobel Prize in Economics, in his book *Human Capital*. "These investments improve skills, knowledge . . . and thereby raise . . . psychic incomes."

Intellectual capital involves how individuals learn over a lifetime and how families communicate, resolve conflict, make joint decisions, and mentor one another. Families need a formal system of representative governance based on articulated family goals and principles to successfully ensure that the family and its members thrive over time.

"Governance can become an anguishing issue," wrote the late Paul N. Ylvisaker, former dean of the Harvard Graduate School of Education and adviser to the Council on Foundations, in *Conscience and Community*, a collection of his essays. "In the first generation, the question is how to overcome the tendency to bow obsequiously to the founding donor; in subsequent generations, how to include a spreading avalanche of family members without being exclusive or overwhelmed."

Social capital refers to an individual's connections with his or her communities. It is a term that has been widely studied in academic circles and has been promoted as "civic engagement" by Robert D. Putnam, Peter and Isabel Malkin Professor of Public Policy at the John F. Kennedy School of Government at Harvard. "Social capital means the features of social life— networks, norms, and trust—that enable participants to act together more effectively to pursue shared objectives," writes Putnam. How does your family interact with our civil society? What are your family members' inclinations for 'civic engagement'? Does your family as a whole (and its individual members) care about others beyond your family?

Financial capital reflects the more traditional definition of wealth, such as the property of the family, its financial assets, trusts, and partnerships, and other investment and estate planning arrangements.

What practical steps can you take to begin designing an effective governance system for your family?

First, hold an initial meeting of your "family assembly" to begin the articulation and documentation of a family "vision" statement. Work in small groups to ask the following questions: What are our family assets? What differentiates our family? Where does our family want to be in 20 years? What shared values do we stand for? Recruit a committee to write a family mission statement and short family history.

"Families throughout the world have created a sense of shared vision and values through the development of a family mission statement," writes Stephen R. Covey in *The 7 Habits of Highly Effective Families*. "The family mission statement is a combined and unified expression of all family members of what your family is about—what it is that you really want to do and be—and the principles you choose to govern your family life." Here is Covey's family mission statement:

> The mission of our family is to create a nurturing place of faith, order, truth, love, happiness, and relaxation, and to provide opportunity for

each individual to become responsibly independent, and effectively interdependent, in order to serve worthy purposes in society.

Second, decide how you will organize yourselves to make decisions. What kind of representative governance structure do you want for your family? How often will you meet as a whole or via small committees made up of family members? What will be on the agendas?

Third, how are you going to educate yourself, your children, and grandchildren over time? I believe the key issues include the following: What does it mean to be an "owner" of financial wealth? What constitutes an effective trustee/beneficiary relationship when family trusts are used to preserve financial wealth? How can children and grandchildren best learn to make competent decisions around financial wealth, family philanthropy, and their legal and investment affairs? How can you help your children discover their calling?

I believe that most productive individuals who contribute to society find a personal calling. For inheritors, this does not mean that they must work for wages, although the family culture may dictate that it is preferable. Work of any kind is important to self-esteem. A recent *New York Times* story on the death of one Harvard graduate captured this point: "And yet his money and his background, or the effect they had on people, conspired to set him apart. He never really found a calling."

"Financial capital alone cannot provide long-term wealth preservation," says Jay Hughes. "What a family's financial capital can provide is a powerful tool to promote the growth of its human and intellectual capital. After all, without human capital, there are no family assets; there is no family! Without intellectual capital, undereducated family members with all the money in the world will not make enough good decisions over a long period of time to outnumber their bad decisions. Successful long-term wealth preservation lies in understanding that it is the growth of a family's human and intellectual capital that determines its success, and that the growth of its financial capital provides a powerful tool to achieve this success."

To expand my understanding of Jay Hughes's philosophy, I interviewed him in Chicago:

COLLIER: Explain the phrase "shirtsleeves to shirtsleeves in three generations."

HUGHES: In every culture that I've encountered—in China, Latin America, and Europe, for example—I run into the same proverb. In China, rice paddy to rice paddy; in Ireland, clogs to clogs.

It appears that financial wealth is destined to disappear in three or four generations. The proverb means that the first generation makes the money, the second generation preserves it, the third generation spends it, and the fourth generation must re-create it.

I prefer the rice paddy idiom; for example, imagine a poor couple in China wearing torn clothing. They pull rice every day and make a financial fortune. They don't leave their home or change their way of life.

The second generation moves to the city, joins the opera board, and becomes significant members of society. The third generation, having no experience of work, spends the money, and the fourth generation goes back to working in the rice paddy.

COLLIER: Why does the third or fourth generation tend to dissipate the family financial wealth?

HUGHES: Basically, they do not learn to work. Work in its deepest dimension equates to a calling. Discovering your calling is the most important task an individual can undertake, and to do this successfully requires that you seek a mentor and become an apprentice to learn what you are called to do and be in life.

Successful families ask the fundamental questions. Who are you? What is your passion? How can I enhance your life journey and your pursuit of happiness? These are the most powerful questions a parent, friend, or mentor can ask. In fact, each generation must in turn re-ask these critical questions around passion and calling.

I believe that the mission of the family is to enhance the individual pursuit of happiness of each family member. Successful individuals keep the entire family growing and thriving. That is the heart of my philosophy, and what I see successful families practicing.

COLLIER: What do you mean by "family governance"?

HUGHES: I am talking about the process of joint decision making. I am convinced that a family, like any endeavor, must develop a way to make decisions, resolve conflicts, and find some level of consensus.

In families that have moved from the sibling generation to the first-cousin generation, you find for the first time large numbers of individuals who didn't grow up in the same household. Thus, you need a structure for those first cousins to be able to form the consensus necessary to make decisions. If you move to second cousins and great-grandchildren, you're now looking at a very diverse set of upbringings. Again, if you then don't have a formal structure for getting together and making decisions, it's very unlikely that they will have much in common—except the family's financial wealth.

If a family wants to survive for a long time, it is critical that it evolve a governance structure appropriate to itself to afford an opportunity to make those decisions that need to be made jointly.

COLLIER: What would be an effective governance structure?

HUGHES: Human beings almost always end up in governance structures with three branches. First, they set up a *family assembly*, which is the policy-making branch to which all members of the family are welcome. In my opinion, the spouses should be included.

Many families then involve the members of the family assembly in committees to carry out the wishes of the family assembly during the period between meetings. Often, one of these committees becomes a form of family executive and is frequently referred to as the *family council*.

The most advanced families create a third branch, the *judicial branch*, establishing a council of elders who resolve disputes, help the family define its vision and mission, remind the assembly when it's not following its rules, and ensure that the family stories are told. (Only elders, who have wisdom and know the family stories, can perform that function.)

COLLIER: What's the role of a family mission statement?

HUGHES: First, let me make a distinction between vision and mission. A shared vision is critical to a family. It is the leap of faith that a family can take together that says, "We are a family, we share a vision of what the family is, and we wish to stay together to perpetuate that vision."

Mission is the carrying out of that vision. It's the expression of the process of the vision. I think that's an important distinction.

Having said that, I believe strongly that if you don't know where you're going, you won't be able to get there. The mission statement for a family is its statement of the direction in which it wishes to go and what kind of family it wants to be. What is frequently missed by families that disappear is that they fail to articulate and share a common vision and the mission that carries it on.

What is critically important is that the mission statement flow downward to all the entities in which the family does things together—for example, in their philanthropic work, their investments, or operation of a family business.

COLLIER: How does a family apply your lessons?

HUGHES: Have a family meeting, and ask a number of critical questions. First, each member should be asked, "What are you passionate about, and who are you to your friends?" Get right to the question of passion. Go to the question of journey.

Second, ask this question: "What's this family going to look like in twenty years?" Work together on what you want your family to do and to stand for in the future.

Talk about forms of family governance. Are you a democracy? Are you a dictatorship? How do you make decisions and resolve conflict? How would you like to make decisions?

The fourth element is learning that with privilege comes responsibility. You have to get used to the responsibilities of the different roles in families, whether it's as a trustee, beneficiary, shareholder, or grantmaker. Each of those roles requires responsibility to obtain the benefits of privilege.

Again, you start with a family meeting and work through those four elements. That way you will create a family that functions well as an enterprise.

COLLIER: Do you think a family should hold one meeting a year?

HUGHES: I think one general meeting a year is absolutely obligatory. By the way, a lot of time at the meeting should be given to telling the family stories. They are the glue. It is through these stories that we learn best who we are as a family.

Do you need to have two or three meetings a year? Maybe. It depends on the work that has to be done. If your family has a number of enterprises, businesses, family trusts, or philanthropic funds, then the family council, for example, may need to meet with the assembly more often than once a year to discuss what needs to be done.

COLLIER: How do children learn to deal with financial wealth?

HUGHES: One of the insights I've gleaned over the years is the fundamental mismatch in people's minds between management and ownership. Every child born into a family of privilege automatically becomes an *owner*. Each becomes a stakeholder in the family as an enterprise, an owner of the heritage of that family and of a portion of the financial wealth.

Every single person in such a family should be taught how to be a great owner, knowing that very few are going to be called to financial careers. Since I believe that financial capital is simply a tool to enhance the growth of the human, intellectual, and social wealth of a family, it follows that human, intellectual, and social wealth can grow only if all the family members understand their roles as owners of the enterprise. They are free to pursue their own calling, but they must accept responsibility as owners of the enterprise that is a family.

Stewardship, to me, is another way of talking about ownership. Many families, in trying to deal with this issue, confuse ownership/ stewardship with management. Management is a science. Ownership, on the other hand, is the art of conserving and stewarding.

COLLIER: What is the role of philanthropy within the governance structure of a family?

HUGHES: I frequently use philanthropy as a learning tool for the operation of various family enterprises. After all, a family philanthropy has to learn to invest because it has an endowment, which must be managed prudently. It has administrative, management, and grant-making components. Therefore, it is a training ground for the basic administrative and management issues that are found in all enterprises.

Most importantly, you have to make joint decisions around the foundation's grants. You have to learn how to create consensus, access requests, listen carefully to the other points of view, and make sound judgments. You learn how to work together. These same lessons apply in all endeavors within the family.

On a deeper level, philanthropy is a way for your family to express its values—for example, the principles of giving back and improving society. Family philanthropy is at the core of what I mean by social wealth, giving to the outside world of your time, talent, and treasure.

CHAPTER 6

Psychological Parenting: Managing Oneself

"Is the financial success of parents detrimental to the development of emotionally healthy, productive children?" asks Dr. Lee Hausner, a Los Angeles–based clinical psychologist and author, in her book, *Children of Paradise: Successful Parenting for Prosperous Families.* "Does high parental achievement put children at risk? Do the hard-won advantages that well-to-do parents are rightfully proud to provide their children automatically create problems that outweigh the benefits? What happens to the basics of good parenting when we add the advantages and disadvantages of wealth and power that come with affluence?"

Most parents would agree that they hope their children will develop into "emotionally stable, competent individuals who can make a contribution to the world," to use Hausner's words. However, the presence of substantial wealth—whether inherited money or sudden wealth—can make parenting even more of a challenge. Do you raise children differently in the context of significant financial wealth?

"While effective parenting is an arduous task for all mothers and fathers, and some parenting pitfalls are universal, affluent parents and their offspring face a unique set of problems," Hausner points out in her book. "Just as poverty has a profound influence, so too does affluence. It creates distinct problems as well as opportunities.

"High-achieving parents often apply the same business skills and acumen at home while raising their children, and they fail to realize that a different set of attitudes and behaviors is necessary to ensure that their children develop into adults with productive and fulfilling lives. An effective parent must be open-minded and willing to question the correctness of their own attitudes, able to admit a mistake, and receptive to new learning. Successful parenting involves a special set of skills and orientation that cannot be directly taken from boardroom behavior."

In fact, the sense of control and insistence on perfection that work well in parents' business lives are often not useful in the family setting. "Children

rtured and encouraged," Hausner points out, "and they need
ι they make mistakes, as well as the willingness to allow them
ιwn choices. Above all, they need opportunities to take charge
ιnd to assume personal responsibility if they are eventually to
ιιιαιιαge their own lives."

Time is a precious commodity in our lives. Many well-meaning parents unintentionally limit their availability to be with their children because of important business, social, and charitable commitments. "While it is not possible to create universal rules regarding time," Hausner says, "learning effective parenting techniques can make the time you spend with your children meaningful, memorable, and special, so that you are, in a sense, with them even when you are not." Many observers have pointed out that the quality of time we spend with our children is just as important as the quantity.

Another challenge in raising children in the context of wealth is how to give them a balanced sense of the role of money in their lives, ensuring that they make the connection between work and reward—that is, the value of money. "If affluent parents do not actively instill within their children a sense of value and respect for money and the effort earning it requires," asserts Hausner in *Children of Paradise*, "the result can be a child who not only believes there is an endless supply of capital but one who consequently abuses it."

Further challenges include being realistic in your expectations of children, helping them to develop their own competencies and thus avoiding unhealthy dependence on the powerful adults surrounding them. You should learn to be an excellent listener, communicating in a manner that demonstrates respect for each child. Finally, take responsibility for a financial parenting program.

People are not born with well-developed parenting skills. Therefore, Hausner suggests that parents commit to a process of learning how to enhance those skills. Participating in a communication workshop or enrolling in a parenting program such as the "Systematic Training for Effective Parenting" (STEP) is an excellent beginning. Additionally, there are many useful parenting guides such as *Children: The Challenge* by Rudolf Dreikurs.

The family is a fluid, continually evolving, emotional system. Each set of relationships (parent to parent, sibling to sibling, parent to child) affects the entire family. In the often-changing world of the affluent family, such issues as financial difficulties, stress-related illness, divorce, and frequent job changes and relocations can all have a significant effect on the interactions within the family system. Parents need to examine their daily actions in terms of the impact they have on the larger context of the family.

To gain a better perspective on these issues, I talked to Katherine Gibson of Charlottesville, Virginia, who heads a consulting firm, The Inheritance Project, Inc., which focuses on the emotional aspects of wealth. She told me about three challenges she and other inheritors have commonly experienced:

> When I was younger, I felt a subtle form of isolation, and this was especially acute after college, when I was working on my own and saw the financial limitations firsthand that most people live with. I had an uneasy sense that I was somehow "different," just because of my money.

> Another experience that I, and many inheritors, have had is guilt— the feeling that you have this money simply because you were born into it. My sense of guilt is now gone, however, because I've actively made good use of the money for my family and for society.

> For some inheritors, the sense of guilt is exacerbated by how the family wealth was acquired, for example, through a tobacco company. Fortunately, that was not the case in my family. My parents' messages around our family business and wealth were positive, and there was always a sense that our family business had a responsibility to its community.

> A third issue is one of empowerment around money. For many inheritors, the money is there for their benefit, but it's not actually theirs since it is often held in trust. It requires a kind of double-mindedness to come to terms with money that is both yours and not yours. The question becomes "How do you form a relationship with money when it's ultimately controlled by someone else?"

> All of these issues have an impact on one's self-esteem. I've worked and feel competent, but I've never had to struggle financially the way other people have to throughout their lives. I am very conscious of these emotional issues and think deliberately how best to raise my two children in regard to our family money.

Lee Hausner and I met in Florida to talk about the most important psychological issues surrounding wealth.

COLLIER: What are the key issues connected with the psychology of money?

HAUSNER: Few people feel comfortable talking about money. It's the last conversational taboo. We discuss everything else, but issues dealing with money cause a variety of negative feelings and so little is usually said. Even the phrase "If you have to ask how much it costs, you can't afford it" reveals the idea that money is not something that we should discuss. Yet money is vital to life and should not be denied. It's something that we need to learn to manage and to deal with strategically. Teaching these skills to the next generation is part of one's parenting responsibility.

Money by itself is no longer just a commodity for barter. It has become a substitute for things such as power, control, love, happiness, and self-esteem. It is basic to our lives, and individuals must learn how to control money and not let it control them. We live in a world of money. Unfortunately, there is insufficient information available regarding its effects on our children or how to use it wisely.

COLLIER: How do you raise productive children who are responsible with wealth?

HAUSNER: I feel that the critical goals for successful child rearing are twofold: to raise a child who is emotionally well-integrated and to raise one who has developed sufficient competency to make a positive contribution to society.

If these are the goals, then the question to be asked is "In what way does money enhance or detract from the ability to create such a child?" Obviously, money enables parents to provide all the basic needs, including wonderful educational and travel opportunities. But the downside is that money can also negate the need for achievement.

If you already have money without the necessity of working, it becomes easy not to develop the discipline and focus that lead to competency. Children who are raised in an impoverished environment are forced to become independent and competent because there is nobody providing for them. Whatever they desire must come through their own effort.

What happens to a wealthy child surrounded by people who do things for the child: tutors, nannies, and strong parents—a whole world of people whose main function is to service this child? When does this child have an opportunity to become competent?

The critical issue is the lack of work experience. If you read autobiographies of great achievers, most of them struggled and had significant work experience. They sold newspapers, they worked on the docks, they worked in a store. They really worked hard, and this type of work is one of the important competency experiences.

Contrast this to the world of wealthy children. If they're not in school, they're often in summer camp or traveling in Europe. Not only do they often miss the opportunity of working, but in families of generational wealth they don't even see the model of work in their families. The source of the family's financial support is a trust fund. In these situations, how are they going to get the idea about what it means to work?

Work is important because it is a method of validating oneself. Additionally, it gives the individual the opportunity to experience the "high" of achievement. When a child becomes addicted to the excitement of achievement, then money will not impair their productivity.

I have had the opportunity of working for the past two years with a number of the new technology millionaires. Many of them come from middle-class backgrounds, and their primary concern is that their newfound riches not destroy the middle-class values that they feel are so important. And when they speak of "middle-class values," they refer to the importance of work and being productive. Because the world of investing, philanthropy, and financially indulging their children is new to them, they are open to learning the skills necessary to effectively handle all aspects of their new wealth.

COLLIER: How do parents provide financial security, yet create opportunities for meaningful work that leads to self-actualization?

HAUSNER: Parents have to give their children opportunities to be competent as often as possible. This means that from the time your children are able to do anything for themselves, they do it. In spite of the consideration that your family may employ full-time help, children need to be assigned specific chores for which they are responsible. These might include setting the table, cleaning their rooms, and feeding pets. Additionally, I think you must stimulate them intellectually. Talk to your children and ask for their opinions.

COLLIER: Entrepreneurial parents have said to me, "I have a seven-year-old child, and we're flying in our private jet to Jackson Hole. I'm worried about the message I'm sending my child. How do I raise children with a balanced view of our family wealth?"

HAUSNER: This is a big challenge. What the parents might say is, "We happen to be extremely fortunate, and we have this jet that we can use on special occasions. Most people are not able to use this airplane, and we do not talk about it because it will make people feel unhappy or jealous. This is a luxury item that is available because your mom or your dad worked very hard."

COLLIER: What if the financial wealth is inherited?

HAUSNER: Then the "script" changes somewhat. What you say is, "We are very lucky because Grandfather or Grandmother worked very hard to create the wealth we enjoy. But very few other people are going to be able to have the advantage of this kind of resource. It means that we need to get ourselves as competent as possible so that we can manage our money well because, if these resources are not managed, we could lose what we have."

COLLIER: What steps can parents take to help their children realize their social responsibility?

HAUSNER: It is critical for families of wealth to expose their children on an active basis to people who are less fortunate so that they have the opportunity to appreciate how fortunate they really are. For example, go to a homeless shelter and spend a morning a month—not just giving money—working with the kids, so that your children get a chance to see how lucky they are.

COLLIER: What can parents do to minimize the "entitlement syndrome"?

HAUSNER: The issue of entitlement is a real concern. It is the issue that Robert Coles discussed in his book, *Privileged Ones: The Well-Off and Rich in America*. He was the first one who really talked about entitlement and how that sense that some children develop that the world owes them can, in fact, cripple them emotionally. (His book came out just about the time I went to work for the Beverly Hills school system.) Parents have got to set limits and tell their children they're not going to get everything they want even if the family can afford it.

COLLIER: When do you think children should receive their financial inheritance?

HAUSNER: I feel strongly that parents should not give their children a significant financial inheritance during their career-building years, say, ages 22 to 35. I don't mean that you shouldn't help them out financially with their needs around health, education, reasonable housing, philanthropy, entrepreneurial activity, and financial education. But in terms of when they are going to receive a large inheritance, it shouldn't be during those important career-building years. I don't think they should get it until they're around 40. They need to make it on their own if they're going to achieve any kind of competence. Money can derail the work they need to do during those critical years.

Building a career is not easy. There are tasks and challenges that most young adults would want to avoid if they could. And often the motivation to stay focused and disciplined in these situations is the actual need to support oneself. Excessive funds make it easy to walk away. But the result of the hard work and effort is the eventual "high" these young adults receive when they achieve on their own. At the end of the day, when your child looks in the mirror and says, "This was a life well led," it will be because they felt they were an achieving individual.

Any time we derail that sense of accomplishment, there is cause for concern, and too much money too soon is a potential for derailment. If career building extends to 40, then I believe they need to make it on their own. The difference with the young "dot-comers" is that they did it themselves; it wasn't given to them. And even if the money "goes to their heads," at least they have earned that right. They know they can achieve.

COLLIER: You don't think parents should fund their children's lifestyles until they're much older?

HAUSNER: Not until they have a chance to make it on their own and have the joy of saying, "I followed my passion and can manage my own life." I am also in favor of supporting children following a passion that is not financially rewarding—like social work or teaching. Parents could, for example, match the earned income so that children making this career choice would not be financially penalized. Making the world a better place could be an important value in your family, and you want to reward that kind of passion.

COLLIER: Should all the children know that Mom and Dad are going to subsidize the social worker in the family?

HAUSNER: Yes. I am a firm believer in family meetings from the time your children are very young. Regular family meetings provide a natural forum for talking about issues like this. In this case, you might have a family discussion about matching earned income up to a certain amount so that all family members would be aware of their options.

Of course, you wouldn't have to match the income of a child who is a successful investment banker, but it is important to talk about it before your children even make those choices. I think you have to talk to your children about these issues before they go to college and start thinking about careers. You might say, "One of the uses of our money is to help you meet a minimal level of economic life. If you want to be a social worker or an artist and you make a career choice based on your passion, which is not financially remunerative such as teaching, social work, or the creative arts, this is what your family will do to support that choice." But it ought to be a match to the amount that your child earns independently.

COLLIER: Should wealthy parents continue to work?

HAUSNER: I have been asked that question by young entre neurs who now have more money than they will spend in lifetimes and want to leave their current job. My response is that, unless at least one parent is working, their children will not see a model of work in their family and may not understand the value in working and being motivated to work themselves. If wealthy parents want a more balanced lifestyle, they can model the "work ethic" of discipline and focus through philanthropic endeavors, a second career, or pursuing an avocation in a professional manner.

COLLIER: Is it possible that financial wealth can derail relationships within the family?

HAUSNER: When money is used as a substitute for parental love, "things" will become very important. If one family member perceives that another is receiving more "things," envy and resentment will derail relationships. However, if a child has a strong sense of self-worth and a genuine feeling of connectedness within the family, then the financial wealth will not disrupt the family.

COLLIER: What is the role for mentors in families?

HAUSNER: Mentors play a vital role. The more positive relationships you can expose your children to—which is really what the mentoring relationship is—the more this child is going to grow and develop. Mentors are often very important in families, because sometimes it is hard for parents to be mentors. Often they're so close they can't separate and they get too involved in the achievement of a child. As a result, they can't be as objective as a mentor can be. The opportunity to be mentored by an aunt, an uncle, or another family member becomes important.

Mentors can be outsiders too. They can help children in business, philanthropy, and career development, for example. Or suppose you have a friend who's just a very wise individual. You may ask that person to mentor your child. What you're doing with a mentor is finding characteristics that you would like your child to be exposed to.

Aunts, uncles, and grandparents have, for years, served as mentors. Very often a child will say, "The most significant influence in my life was my grandfather, who had the time to talk with me and taught me important things about life." These are wonderful mentoring relationships.

COLLIER: What do you think about prenuptial agreements?

HAUSNER: I believe in a prenuptial agreement because healthy relationships should not be based on finances. A prenuptial agreement is a business contract, and with the high rate of divorce that occurs, families should protect the business or financial assets of the family. It protects wealth that was created before the marriage. Signing a prenuptial clearly indicates that money is not the motivation for this marriage.

I think the problem with prenuptials is that the parties involved are not able to discuss it in a comfortable way. Often, the concept of a prenuptial has never been discussed until someone comes home engaged. Obviously, there will be apprehension when this proposition is presented to the other party.

Families of wealth should talk about prenuptials from the time of their children's adolescence. They need to explain the importance of the wealth-protection philosophy of the family and how this will enable the financial wealth to grow for future generations as well as providing lifetime benefits to the current generation. Family money should have nothing to do with the love between two individuals who wish to marry. When discussing this idea with future in-laws, it is important to emphasize that, even with a prenuptial, everyone will benefit from this type of financial wealth preservation. There can be trips, vacation homes, educational trusts for children, and retirement security, for example. The prenuptial doesn't take any of that away. Additionally, the new couple will have the full benefits of the wealth that they create together, and this should be seen as a priority.

COLLIER: What about family philanthropy?

HAUSNER: Philanthropy is an important part of the social capital of a family. Parents should be clear in transmitting the message that when a family is fortunate enough to have significant wealth, there is an obligation to give back to society and that part of the financial wealth transfer planning of this family will involve charitable giving. This is an important message to give children and helps them to include the needs of others.

COLLIER: What is the role for philanthropy in helping children to become competent?

HAUSNER: One of the benefits of philanthropy is that it involves collective problem solving around grant-making activity and gives family members an active experience of how to be cooperative and collaborative.

I think they also have a chance to become educated financially. You can talk more easily about assets that don't belong to the family but are going to be used to improve society. The great thing about philanthropy is that children are often exposed to other mentors, people who are philanthropic.

COLLIER: Finally, why is it important to think about the psychological issues around family wealth? What is really at stake for families and for the individual members?

HAUSNER: There is a lot at stake because you don't want to leave the development of your children to chance. You need to be strategic, develop a plan, and tell your children explicitly what they can expect in the future.

The message in my family was "I expect you to take care of yourself, to earn your own way, and to support yourself when you're out of college." That was a very clear message. My two children never thought they were going to come home and live indefinitely. They just never even considered any other option because that was the message we gave them.

We also gave them the best education they could have, and we said they could stay in graduate school as long as they wanted. That was the rule. As long as they're in school, they get funded. The minute they are not in school, they don't get funded. This is their life, and I'm not going to foster lengthy dependency. It's time for independence. Graduation day is independence day. I believe you provide them with all the tools they need to achieve. That is one joy of having money: you can give your children all the tools that they need to be competent and independent adults.

CHAPTER 7

Financial Parenting: Managing Money

"We did some financial education indirectly over time with our children when they were young," says John F. Keane, Sr., chairman and former CEO of Boston-based Keane, Inc., a leading IT software consulting company. "More recently, we talked about financial education directly when we set up trusts for our three children and gave them some money outright. The money is at risk, but their ability to use their judgment and experiment with it is part of their learning curve. I believe it's a good idea to think and talk about financial education for your family."

Today, it is easy to conclude that financial education for your family is a must. After all, financial education is a form of your family's human capital that needs to be enhanced over a lifetime. There is too much at stake to leave the "basic training" about money to chance and hope that your children will absorb pertinent information by osmosis.

Kathryn M. McCarthy, director of client advisory services at Rockefeller & Company in New York, says financial education is critical. "It facilitates the preservation of the family's financial wealth," says McCarthy, explaining why you should take educating the next generation seriously. "Today, we are inundated with financial information and advice—good and bad—and we all need to be conversant in the basics of wealth management in order to interpret the information and to ask good questions. This is especially true for all members of wealthy families.

"It's a part of your life. You have to become financially savvy sooner because the world is more sophisticated. Money is a hot topic, and there's more information that is coming faster, especially on the Internet. Moreover, enlightened advisers are willing to bring family members—even if they are young or lack experience—into the picture. They know that all family members have a stake in decisions about money."

How do you give your children the skills to manage inherited wealth? How do you best prepare them to handle an inheritance? What should you do in the way of financial education? Raising financially responsible children isn't easy—either for children or for parents—and yet the stakes are high. If wealth holders want their children to become competent in using their financial inheritance wisely, then I believe they should implement a financial education program and tailor it to the *individual* needs of their children. There is much to learn about saving, spending, philanthropy, working with investment professionals, understanding trusts, and personal budgeting.

Here are four things you can do to get started: set an example, provide guidance, allow consequences, and use mentors.

Set a good example

Most developmental psychologists say that our parental modeling has a powerful influence on our children's behavior, even if not immediately. Some have asserted that the way parents talk with each other about money is also important. Therefore, the first step toward instilling a sense of financial responsibility regarding family wealth is your own example and the messages you send to your children by your behavior with money. How should we act? For starters, we ought to exhibit prudent spending habits, put some limits on luxuries, talk about the economic aspects of family life, and tell our children why and where we are philanthropic. These positive practices send children profound signals about money and its role in our lives. Thoughtful parental modeling around spending and philanthropy will positively affect our children.

"Of course, parents have to be positive role models," adds McCarthy. "First of all, they need to understand their own family history around money and how well or poorly *their* parents performed as role models. For example, I recently talked to a middle-aged woman who had never written a check. Her husband took care of the family finances, as was the case in her mother's generation. She was recently widowed and now has to deal with valuable stock options from her husband's estate. Despite a good education, she patterned herself financially like her mother. It will take an enormous effort for this woman now to be able to understand recommendations from her advisers and the consequences of that advice."

Provide consistent guidance

A deliberate plan of financial education is just as important as your example in ensuring that your children learn to handle their inheritance properly. Handling money well is a life skill that is best learned gradually over time. As children grow older, they can take on more responsibility and handle sophisticated financial tasks and concepts.

You can begin early, for example, at age 5 to 7 with an allowance. Even something as simple as an allowance raises sharp questions. Should an allowance be a payment for chores? What are the consequences if they do not do the chores required for the allowance? What is a responsible amount?

Here is a list of age-appropriate steps you can take to educate children:

Grade school, ages 6 to 12

- Discuss caring for possessions.

- Structure an allowance: Most experts suggest a modest amount for being part of the family and doing certain basic household chores.

- Provide jobs for pay.

- Encourage long-term savings: Consider matching any money they will save for over a year.

- Set limits around money, for example, not buying everything they want when you go shopping.

- Introduce philanthropy: Help them to give and take them on site visits.

Teen years, ages 13 to 18

- Insist on summer employment; fund their Roth IRA.

- Guide them through their budget and a 1040 tax return.

- Advocate smart consumerism: For example, discuss the messages in advertising and the impact of advertising on their purchases.

- Discuss the intelligent use of credit cards and checking accounts.

- Explore investments on the Internet.

- Engage them in philanthropy: Encourage site visits and include them in evaluating gift decisions.

s, ages 18 and over

th them on a college spending budget.

summer employment and fund their Roth IRA.

- Set up adviser-facilitated learning about investments.

- Provide money for them to manage.

- Explain the roles of trustee and beneficiary, if trusts are used in your family.

- Engage them in philanthropy; add them to the board of your philanthropic fund.

Allow them to make mistakes

Let your children make mistakes with their own money, such as spending money on toys that go out of fashion or break immediately. It's often a mistake for us to bail them out when they make bad decisions. Help them understand what they still have to learn or what they might do differently. Children need to learn early and often that they are responsible for their decisions, including those that involve money, and must live with the consequences.

"I think young adults in their early twenties should have some money ($10,000 to $20,000) and be told it is theirs to do with as they please," argues McCarthy. "They should be allowed to spend it, invest in their friends' movies or Internet companies, for example, and possibly lose it. And if they make mistakes, they can learn how to deal with the consequences—both financial and personal—such as losing a friend or trusting the wrong person. Mistakes with money can be an important learning experience, but they can also provide an opportunity to discuss what went right or wrong—while avoiding blame or embarrassment."

Consider the use of mentors

Businesses have had formal mentoring programs for years and have found that this kind of executive "coaching" can be very successful. Applying the same strategy to financial education in families with wealth can also be effective.

"Studies show that caring teachers and firm, wise coaches greatly influence the course of many young lives," says John R. O'Neil, president of the

Center for Leadership Renewal in California in his book, *The Paradox of Success*. "Once out of school, we largely do without the aid of teachers, but the need remains. They (mentors) can be supportive yet objective, using their outside perspective to help you see the larger pattern of your development."

As mentioned in the last chapter, mentors can be family members (aunts, uncles, grandparents, for example) or nonfamily outsiders such as teachers, advisers, or friends. The arrangement can be formal or informal. Mentors provide a rich apprenticeship experience, educating young people on financial matters, helping with personal and career aspirations, furthering their long-term learning, and supporting them when they fail. The important point is not to overlook the option of mentors as a way to provide the financial education you desire for members of your family.

"My parents' generation thought a lot about how to raise responsible children," says William Weil, an executive vice president of the National Geographic Ventures in Washington, D.C. He explains that the older generation realized that if they wanted the younger generation to be responsible, they had to give them responsibility first:

> Responsibility took many forms, including communicating the details about the family's wealth, ongoing financial education, granting limited investment decisions (where mistakes could be made), and learning about and participating in family philanthropy.

> The education around family investments and philanthropy for me and my 16 cousins and siblings started seriously as soon as we each reached age 18. Our parents were clear about the dual purpose of the wealth: to enable us to live well while pursuing diverse careers and to allow us to support causes we cared about.

> Now everyone has an equal understanding of what's happening with the investments in their trusts, while recognizing that people are different and some are less interested in the financial education. What's been helpful to us is the openness and communication around the money and its management.

I asked Kathryn McCarthy to expand on the issue of how a family can start a program of financial education for children. A financial adviser trained as a lawyer and also in finance, she has served the family offices of the Rockefellers and Sulzbergers. She conducts financial education programs for individuals and families throughout the United States.

COLLIER: Why should families undertake a program of financial education for their family members?

MCCARTHY: I think the first question is: Should families talk about their wealth at all? Should families develop a philosophy about their wealth before deciding what kind of financial education to create? Is financial education useful?

It's been my experience that if families focus on what the money means—creating more wealth for future generations or undertaking family philanthropy, for example—these families develop the necessary values around money that can be articulated to current and future generations.

Developing a core set of values around the use of money contributes to the overall health of the family and sustains it through many financial decisions. If there is no discussion, then they may be denying a part of who they are as a family.

So before we ask the question "Why financial education?" we need to ask whether families should talk about money in general and what money means to them as a prelude to financial parenting.

COLLIER: Why do children in wealthy families need financial education when investment professionals are available to them?

MCCARTHY: There are many reasons. First, society presumes that they know something about their money. They have to operate in a world that is fueled—rightly or wrongly—by financial considerations. It's expected of them.

But, more importantly, knowing the way financial, legal, and trust matters work actually helps the family communicate. Family members can develop a common and often unique way of looking at their finances. I've experienced families who develop their own language as a way to express financial and legal concepts.

Financial education also allows family members to maintain their individuality because, if they want to build on the knowledge, they can do so. I see financial education as a way to foster family harmony and to promote family communication.

COLLIER: Are you saying that some base of knowledge puts all the children on an equal footing?

MCCARTHY: Yes, and that's another reason why financial education is important. Families and their structures around money change. There are deaths, births, divorces, investment windfalls, and financial reverses. Ultimately, the family as a whole has to take responsibility for their money. It's understanding that with the wealth come opportunity and responsibility. One of the responsibilities of being a wealth owner is to be educated about your money.

The kind of education that I'm referring to is basic financial knowledge, including information surrounding personal finance, investment management, and legal structures that allow you to follow a conversation about your wealth and ask questions of people who advise you with confidence.

Wealthy individuals are typically supported by a series of advisers, either outside professionals or the staff of their family office. Therefore, individual family members must have enough knowledge to assess whether the advice is relevant, timely, and appropriate. You can't do that in a vacuum; you need to develop at least the sense of what's going on in the financial world at large and in the family's financial environment. My experience is that almost everyone in a family is called on, at some time, to be a part of decisions about the family money, and they need to prepare for that.

COLLIER: Who should provide the financial education?

MCCARTHY: In my view, the parents should initiate the process with their children at a young age. I was recently with a family psychologist who said that she never heard any complaints about people giving information too early. But she had scores of stories about the problem of giving the information too late.

The trusted adviser and, often, the family office can continue the groundwork laid by parents. I know a couple with bright young children who were interested in the stock market. The parents had their investment adviser talk to the children about stocks and bonds. The children are now investing in mutual funds and getting information online.

Many families have formal education programs that are often held around family meetings. I recommend that parents include outside advisers in the process so that the next generation becomes accustomed to the way advisers work and the different kinds of advice they give. There also should be different faces in front of a next generation, not just the *parents'* advisers.

I have a situation where I'm a trustee of a trust for the sole purpose of educating the next generation, and I am not an adviser to the senior family members. This was a conscious decision and has worked with great success.

I view financial education as a journey, and there are a number of phases. It begins when children are young, answering the "what is" questions and defining concepts like stocks, bonds, philanthropy. It moves to the teenage years, answering the "how to" questions such as how one invests or makes grants. In adulthood, the "integration" question comes up; for example, how does an investment program fit in with various family trusts? Sometimes it's not until they are 40 or 50 that they see how it all fits together.

There are also education programs sponsored by institutions like the Council on Foundations. These are devoted to educating family members. There are conferences, workshops, summer camps, and retreats on financial education. Parents want their children to be educated, and many understand that they can't do it all and that their advisers sometimes are not the appropriate people.

COLLIER: Is there a role for grandparents?

MCCARTHY: Yes, grandparents are an excellent resource. They have financial wisdom through experience, even if they lack technical expertise. They are good teachers, having practiced on their children. I've often observed a kind of magic when grandparents teach young children financial concepts.

COLLIER: Who is this financial education for: parents, children, grandchildren?

MCCARTHY: Financial education is for everyone. We focus on the younger generation because they often need it the most. Spouses and in-laws are important too. One way to get in-laws

involved is to have them be part of an educational program
themselves can learn and transmit knowledge in a differen'
the family members.

Financial education is for the whole family. This may souna
trite, but the family that learns together is going to have a way of
communicating with one another and can become stronger by the
common experience.

The older wealth holders—and the newer "dot-com entrepreneurs"—need to be careful not to be so busy making the money
that they don't take the time to transmit some level of knowledge
to their family members. If they can't learn together, they should
inspire the next generation to learn on their own. Wealthy families have a wonderful opportunity to do this because they have the
resources to make it happen.

COLLIER: At what age do you start financial education?

MCCARTHY: Neale Godfrey has written a useful book, *A
Penny Saved*, suggesting you should start at age three. I think you
can start early—at age five or so—with simple concepts like saving, spending, and giving. One can't begin a program based on
age alone. The program must be tailored to the learning style and
ability of the child. It's important, particularly in a larger multigenerational family, to have family members of similar ages learning together.

**COLLIER: What about the teenage years and the use of the
Internet?**

MCCARTHY: We have a fabulous opportunity with teenagers
because the Internet is a tool they really understand. There are
hundreds of great websites like Motley Fool that have all kinds
of information and interactive programs for teenagers. It seems
that more sites are being developed daily. Teenagers especially
need this resource because it enables them to learn on their own.
It's empowering for them to learn at a pace tailored to their own
learning style. But they're not going to get everything off the
Internet, and it can be isolating. Make sure they have access to
other forms of learning with their peers and from other individuals.

In some of the programs I've held for wealthy families, I approach it like teaching a class. There was a group of 16- and 17-year-olds and 18- and 19-year-olds. They worked together and reinforced one another's learning. The learning has to be fun, relevant, and at a level they can understand.

COLLIER: What kind of financial education works well with twentysomethings?

MCCARTHY: Working with children in college or in their twenties can be tricky because of the time constraints and distance. They're going to graduate school, starting careers, and traveling, for example, and therefore organized programs may not be the best vehicles for financial learning.

Individually structured programs and mentoring, in addition to regularly scheduled programs, can be the most important way to reach this age group. For example, let's take the 25-year-old woman living in Boulder whose family is in New York. Her parents' adviser could help her to design a program, which includes finding a mentor, a professor at the University of Colorado, or a local lawyer, for example, along with a plan for attending night programs or lunch discussions at a brokerage firm.

There are a lot of new communication tools for families: conference calls, email, and family websites. Information about programs can be posted on a family website or through email from another family member—for example, "This is what we're thinking about doing, and we're going to have a meeting on the new family partnership or the subject of asset allocation. What kind of information do you need from me or the family office?"

COLLIER: How can parents be realistic about financial education for their children?

MCCARTHY: You start the education early because you may lose them in their teenage years. Once children go out into the world and are subject to peer pressure, you can't expect them to adhere to a program of financial education. They can be more critical and often tend to follow their friends because they don't want to be different. But in the normal course of development, they typically come back in their twenties and see the value of the education.

COLLIER: When do you conclude the financial education for your children?

MCCARTHY: I don't think you ever stop because the family system and its needs are always changing. In many cases, the financial status of the family may remain static for years and then change dramatically for whatever reason: births, deaths, or divorces.

If one can learn key concepts—what is inflation, what is a trust—basic information is formed like a foundation on which a house can be built. For example, a family may not want trusts, but, if there is a disabled child, the need may arise. Having some familiarity with trusts would allow a more focused discussion on the issue of trustee selection and the use of a trust in this situation.

And remember, I'm talking about financial education in the sense of ownership of wealth and being able to ask good questions. It doesn't mean your children have to be able to trade stocks and bonds, draft a will, or know the technical components of a family limited partnership.

COLLIER: Does the family philanthropic fund offer a place for financial education for children?

MCCARTHY: Yes. It's an ideal place to begin and continue financial education because there is an investment and financial component to a family's philanthropic program. A foundation, for example, can serve as an educational tool for teaching investment concepts as well as the financial concept of budgeting.

The philanthropy program is also a great way to engage individuals in the younger generations who don't typically have any say in the overall governance of the family yet. The next generation can receive financial training and observe the way financial decisions are made and their impact by participating in the family philanthropic fund.

I'm currently involved with a family foundation where, for the younger generation to move into a broader role in the family business, they had to demonstrate that they could successfully manage the process of giving away money. They had to know how to budget for grants, understand the foundation's investment program, and communicate with their advisers. It was a wonderful microcosm of what they would ultimately have to do in running their family business. Family philanthropy can provide the beginnings of an individual's understanding of the decision-making process and how different financial disciplines integrate with one another—for example, investments and taxes, or budgeting and investments.

It's also a way for younger family members to learn to appreciate what money means. Many families are unwilling, at certain ages, to tell the complete financial picture to their children and yet are willing to discuss information about the foundation's assets and goals. In fact, the foundation is typically a source of family legacy and pride.

COLLIER: There's a lot of information out there. How much financial information should you give your children?

MCCARTHY: The minimal amount of financial education would be the equivalent of what you would learn in a course on personal finance. Those courses include something on income taxes, the economy, investments, insurance, trusts, estate planning, and the various legal entities that are used in wealth transfer—limited partnership interests and forms of corporations, for example. You also need to know the basic tools and definitions surrounding charitable vehicles.

COLLIER: Are there other skills that children need to learn that are related to financial education?

MCCARTHY: I can think of several. Part of financial education involves some training on the skills of how to make joint decisions and resolve conflicts. In a business sense, this means knowing how to negotiate. Negotiation is a part of business and financial life, and it's certainly an important part of communicating within families. Family members need to understand something about the art of negotiation. There are wonderful books out there— *Getting to Yes* by Roger Fisher, for example—where you are given fundamental ideas on to how to negotiate and influence decisions.

Also, many family members will have to make a presentation at some time to a charity, at their family meeting, or even to the public. Gaining the competence to deliver presentations is another useful skill. Think about the financial people whom you admire; they are all fairly articulate speakers.

These are life skills, and they relate to financial education. Some family members might like to work on these skills before they tackle financial concepts, so this approach can be a way of engaging family members who are not necessarily drawn into financial subject matter.

COLLIER: What have other families done in the way of financial education?

MCCARTHY: Many families have a formal education committee that deals with the family's financial education at all levels, from the seniors down to the 5-year-olds. As part of their family meeting, the education committee reports on programs that they've structured during the course of the year. In fact, part of the family meeting is typically devoted to an hour of financial education for all generations.

I know a family that set up an investment club for their teenagers and younger adult family members. The investment club has a chairman and meets quarterly. Initially, the members attended a two-day intensive program about investments. Each family member was given a research assignment and made decisions about stocks. Their results were measured, which was a hot topic of discussion within the family. Theirs was a true success story.

Education at family meetings can be useful. It's a great time to present a new concept around the family's overall estate planning, such as the creation of a family limited partnership. This gives the family as a whole a chance to learn about the new legal structure, understand terms and expected outcomes, and ask questions. There can also be follow-up information during the year as the plan is put into effect.

COLLIER: How does a family know whether it's been successful with a program of financial education?

MCCARTHY: The family needs to constantly reassess its program. The critical measurement is your family's ability to make decisions as a group about a common financial issue and not leave anyone out of the process because they don't know enough to participate. Being inclusive in family financial discussions is a big indicator. Each family member should have the satisfaction of being able to ask a good question of an adviser and have the answer given in an appropriate adult manner.

Another way of defining success is to look at your family philanthropy. A foundation that is run well in the eyes of the senior and junior generations of the family is an indicator. Remember that the family's philanthropic fund is the "think tank," a tool for charitable giving and financial training.

Finally, I think the most important element is to assess the education along the way. I see programs, often designed by family offices, that are not successful because the family or the family office staff didn't say, "Give me some feedback. Is this educational program working? Does it address your individual needs?"

Successful families understand that they are always learning, that there is no magic solution, and that people learn in different ways. There should be no point at which a family stops trying different things, and, if they make financial education fun, interactive, and continual, it will succeed. Ultimately, success is when the artist in the family is comfortable with a discussion of the family's financial assets and shows up for the meeting!

CHAPTER 8

Philanthropic Parenting: Managing Financial Care

Philanthropy can instill a sense of responsibility around wealth in the next generation of your family. "The more money you have personally," said Bob Stone, "the more responsibility you have to society. Providing an inheritance to our children also gives *them* certain responsibilities as well, including using their wealth to have a positive impact on society."

Family philanthropy (organized charitable giving involving the donor and/or relatives of the donor) can be an effective parenting tool with many benefits. Including your children and grandchildren in charitable giving decisions—even with small amounts of money—can help them in developing the following skills: understanding financial concepts such as investment management, due diligence, and analytical evaluation; learning to work together, make joint decisions, and solve problems; and even public speaking. Moreover, you can emphasize core values, such as generosity and volunteerism, and encourage their individuality through their own giving. Philanthropy can be a competency experience for children, and they can be introduced to the process in their early teenage years.

"Families need to think about involving their children no later than their teenage years, because otherwise you may lose them until they are around thirty," says Virginia M. Esposito, founding president of the National Center for Family Philanthropy in Washington, D.C. "What can you do? Expose them to board meetings, create a junior board that recommends grants, take them on age-appropriate site visits, and encourage them to volunteer. Think of yourself as a mentor helping them to understand their own social commitment. After all, someone inspired you. Finally, tell them why you give and about the satisfaction you experience with your own charitable giving."

Philanthropy can also strengthen your family as a whole. Many families state that their family philanthropy is not only rewarding but has brought them closer together. Paul Ylvisaker described the benefit this way in his article, "Family Foundations: High Risk, High Reward," in the *Family Business Review:*

The returns on a family investment in philanthropy are—or can be—extremely high, both internally and externally. When such an investment is well executed, a family can achieve the cohesion that comes with a sense of higher purpose and cooperative effort. Family members report an excitement and fulfillment going far beyond what they had known as related members of a tribe. Accepting the challenge and educational experience involved in assessing public needs and evaluating grant proposals from the point of view of the public interest is an incomparable experience and one that can build strong bonds among family members.

Virginia Esposito agrees with Ylvisaker and expands the role of the family philanthropic fund: "In my experience, family philanthropies have goals for both family and for society. If you understand that, then you can attend to both. There is often a healthy tension between the two. Your family philanthropy is not just about giving, and it's not just about family. The benefit for your family is the experience of working together on something larger than yourselves, producing a different kind of family engagement and meaning. For younger family members, it expands their horizons about what is possible in the world. The benefit to society is having private money invested in a public purpose."

"Our family foundation gets us together and keeps us connected, even if only by speakerphone!" says Jennifer P. Stone, director of oncology at Nashoba Deaconess Hospital in Concord, Massachusetts, and daughter of Bob Stone. She continues:

> My generation is a diverse group, and we lobby for the causes we care about. I want to support education and the environment and last year directed a gift to the Quebec Labrador Foundation, an international community development and conservation organization I had worked for during college.

> My siblings and I are trying to assess the effectiveness of the gifts to a variety of causes—from providing access to Outward Bound to funding research on Lou Gehrig's disease. We're all on email and do some of the research on the Web.

> We often disagree on the best strategy to leverage our family giving. Will a large gift to a charter school be effective? How does it help society? We're also discussing ways to measure outcomes. We don't have a formal evaluation plan, but we're working on it.

To organize your family philanthropy intelligently, I suggest you explore the following four areas: defining your core values, choosing a giving vehicle, making grants, and transferring leadership.

Defining your core values

Deciding on what you want to accomplish is the first step in planning your family philanthropy. What values does your family stand for? Can these principles guide your family philanthropy? These questions suggest that a discussion of what values, principles, and virtues your family can agree on may help inform and focus your family's philanthropic priorities. To what extent does your family share a set of core values while still making room for individual preferences? (As couples, you may want to work through a short questionnaire, and I have included sample family questionnaires in Appendix B.)

Families have used a number of exercises to help determine the scope of their philanthropy. For example, you can ask each family member to tell a family story that illustrates a value or principle that they care about most. Alternatively, pass out a list of values—honesty, fairness, compassion, respect, commitment, accountability, justice, generosity, spirituality, and personal achievement, for example—and see if a consensus emerges around a few core principles that might shape a focus for your family philanthropy. What kinds of organizations do we want to support or which social issues should we address that reflect our core values? Of course, a formal set of shared values or articulated focus may not be that important to you or your family, but the *conversation* you have with your family members around principles may be useful.

"Once you involve family, you have to ask, 'What do you stand for,'" says Esposito, explaining the value for families of articulating the purpose of their philanthropy and writing a mission statement. "Does everyone who is involved understand and share a common commitment? You should answer these questions before you begin to think of a mission statement for your family philanthropy. This is a 'statement' to your family, friends, and the public describing what your giving is about. It needn't handcuff you or restrict your reach, but it provides a shared sense of purpose. Its greatest value may be the conversation it produces within your own family."

Choosing a giving vehicle

The choice of a legal structure for your family's philanthropy should follow deliberation of what you want to accomplish and why. Esposito elaborates:

> Other good questions to ask about family philanthropy include the following: Whom do you want to involve? Why involve them and how? Once you answer why and how to involve your children and what your grantmaking interests might be, then you can decide whether to have a private foundation or not, whether to have a process for giving or not.
>
> Many families choose multiple charitable vehicles. For example, they might use a private foundation, a donor advised fund, a supporting organization, or no structure at all. I've seen families that use staff, advisers, and research. I've also seen wealthy donors simply write checks.

Most wealth holders use one or more of the following legal entities: private family foundation, supporting organization, or donor advised fund. The private family foundation provides a donor and his or her family complete control over the grant making and investment management, while the supporting organization allows the donor and family shared control. Family members must constitute a minority of the board of a supporting organization. The donor advised fund provides individuals and families with advisory influence without investment and administrative worries.

All of these vehicles have similar benefits. You are allowed to make income- and/or estate-tax-deductible gifts to an entity while retaining the ability to influence or control—to varying degrees—how and when the funds are distributed.

Making grants

To be effective, families have a number of decisions to resolve around their grant making. Here is a preliminary list of the critical questions that you may find useful in discussing philanthropy with your family.

Goals and strategy

- What issues will be the focus of your family's philanthropy?

- Do you want to help solve immediate social problems, invest for long-term change, or both?

- What is your theory of change?

Engagement

- Do you want to be proactive or reactive to issues, that is, a capital provider or an engaged partner?

- Do you want to give independently or collaboratively with other funders?

- Do you want to support established organizations, seed new projects, or both?

Assessment of grantees

- Who will undertake your due diligence research and site visits?

- What questions will you ask to assess the organization's leadership, expertise, financial strength, and chances of success?

Grant making

- What will be the size of your grants?

- Will they be one-time or multiyear grants?

- Will you fund unrestricted support, specific projects, grassroots innovation, or research?

Measuring outcomes

- What will be your criteria to effectively assess the success of your grants?

- How will you know if you have been successful?

- Should you commit money to measure outcomes?

"What do you want to know and why?" says Christine W. Letts, the Rita E. Hauser Lecturer in the Practice of Philanthropy and Nonprofit Leadership at the John F. Kennedy School of Government, discussing the issue of evaluation. "If you want to measure outcomes, you can hire an expert to undertake science-based evaluation and get a report. But the critical question is: What will you do then? Will the evaluation of performance inform your decision-making process?"

Transferring leadership

Should a family philanthropic fund continue past the donor's generation or go out of business? If it is going to be maintained long term, how do you plan the succession of leadership? This is an issue that should be explored early on in the life of your family's philanthropic fund. The question is especially important for families who have made a commitment to a private foundation with substantial resources. There are compelling arguments on both sides.

On the pro side, a family philanthropic fund that lasts for multiple generations has the potential to provide a legacy where your family works together. Since many individuals who create foundations involve their children early on, they are often optimistic about the next two generations' ability to make thoughtful decisions.

A case can also be made for stewarding financial resources to solve *tomorrow's* social problems. I heard one funder say that "foundations are designed to put long-term money toward solving long-term societal problems. They balance other forms of giving that are more immediate."

The argument against perpetuity for a family foundation often rests on the question of public policy: Given the modest 5 percent payout requirement, are private foundations skewed to future generations? Should foundations give more today to solve pressing social needs as opposed to enhancing asset growth for tomorrow? There is also the question of the inevitable shift in donor intent. Many foundations are unable to adhere to the founding donor's intent, given changing family situations and new issues in society. Some families decide that making a significant impact now is more important than existing in perpetuity.

"If you arrange for your wealth to be available in the year 2100, rather than addressing current social needs, the funds may be dispersed in a manner that the long-forgotten donor cannot possibly anticipate by expressions of intent," asserts Gustave M. Hauser, a proponent of a "sunset provision" for foundations. "Many would be well advised to give away most of the money during their lifetimes or require that all funds must be spent within a specific time frame—for example, twenty-five years."

Given the variety of private family foundations in terms of size, staff, and program, the answer to this question will vary greatly. Solutions that others have chosen to resolve the issues concerning foundation longevity include the following:

1. Keep the foundation going and trust the succeeding generations to make effective and responsible decisions.

2. Bring on a substantial number of outside trustees to professionalize the board.

3. Include a specific provision in the foundation's charter to "sunset" or dissolve the foundation (after 20 years or the grandchildren's generation, for example).

4. Allow family members or trustees to determine later whether the foundation will continue long term.

5. Fold the foundation's assets into a community foundation or into one or more nonprofit institutions, or convert it to multiple donor advised funds for individual family members.

6. Hire outside staff to have your foundation evolve into a public operating foundation.

(For an excellent book on succession planning, see Kelin Gersick's *Generations of Giving*, as listed in the bibliography.) "Succession planning for your family philanthropic fund is a serious issue," says Virginia Esposito. She adds:

Once you get to the third generation, maintaining family cohesion is often difficult. Geographical dispersion, lack of shared values, conflicting influence of spouses, and absence of the founder all contribute to possible abandonment of family philanthropy. Like the succession planning for any enterprise, you have to plan and continually ask, "What do we want to accomplish?"

You also need a structure and shared values that make it easy for everyone to stay committed: (1) inspire them to participate, (2) train them to be able to participate, and (3) plan how they will participate when there are, for example, more than 35 cousins involved. In short, how are you going to empower them and involve them when they all can't be on the board? Many families don't think about the issues of succession and perpetuity of their foundation until it's too late and an emergency arises—for example, when Mom or Dad dies. You have to find a way to think about the issue now.

There is something very special about the commitment of a group of people to one another when they share an equally heartfelt commitment to something greater than themselves. There is great passion and compassion.

What follows are some brief narratives from Harvard alumni who have been thoughtful and effective in managing their individual and family philanthropy.

- **Robert R. Barker.** "I set up the JMR Barker Foundation, our private family foundation, over thirty years ago," recalled the late Bob Barker, former general partner of the New York investment firm Barker, Lee and Co. "My primary motivation was involving our children. I wanted them to see how much fun it is to give."

    Bob had been an active philanthropist throughout his life and has made generous gifts to many causes—Harvard College and the American Museum of Natural History among them. However, the focus of his family's foundation giving had been on venture philanthropy. In an interview with the author in 2000, Bob explained his family's approach:

    "We've put up money to research specific problems in Central America, for example, to help preserve the rain forest in the Amazon Basin, and to start a telecommunications program in Eritrea. We have translated the venture capital model from my business to our family philanthropy. We've taken lots of risks; some grants have not worked out, but others have produced bigger rewards. Besides the colleges, schools, and museums we care about, we have, for example, supported the following: the North Atlantic Salmon Federation; Jackson Laboratories; Americares; Life Span Systems; Prep for Prep; the Vermont Land Trust; Tibetan U.S. Resettlement; and the original planning for modernizing Grand Central Terminal.

    "We don't have a staff or a specific focus. The only criterion is that one of the trustees must know the cause or institution intimately. There are ten trustees: six family members and four outsiders drawn from friends, advisers, or business associates. The balance of the trustees is always with the family, and all of my children are on the board.

"We meet twice a year to make grant decisions and discuss the investment results of the foundation. One of the benefits of our foundation is that it has been a vehicle to teach my children about investments, because the agenda of our meetings covers the foundation's portfolio. So they have learned over time.

"Regarding our succession plan, I can say that I have just resigned as chairman of the foundation and my son, Jim, has taken over. Also, my granddaughter, Margaret, a consultant at Trilogy in Austin, Texas, has just joined the board. She's very excited and has ideas and causes that she wants to support, including a project in Boston to enhance wheelchair sports. She wants to keep the foundation going.

"This foundation has been a major force for our family. It's been a wonderful focus twice a year, bringing the family together to discuss causes that are most important to us, individually and collectively. It's been a thrill for me and my children."

Bob's son, Ben Barker, former president and CEO of Data Race, Inc., a communications products company in San Antonio, agrees that the family aspect of their foundation has been important. "The foundation has caused our family to stay in touch, whereas without it we might not see each other," says Ben. "For me, the two most valuable reasons for having a foundation are these: First, it helps the family dynamic by bringing us together; and second, it forces us to think about how to make the world a better place through the institutions we care passionately about. I don't think we would have invested the time and effort and resources without the focus of the foundation."

- **John F. Keane, Sr.** "I started thinking seriously about the meaning of our wealth at a symposium at Harvard Business School a few years ago," says John F. Keane, Sr., in explaining why he and his wife, Marilyn, decided to create a family foundation. "We broke into small groups to discuss 'What is family?' and I came to the conclusion that what is most important is the perpetuation of core values. Eventually, we decided that one way for us to perpetuate our values was to engage our children in a process—family philanthropy—whereby we would discuss and debate how to give away money effectively."

Working with their three grown children and their children's spouses, the Keanes developed a foundation mission statement to reflect their deep interest in helping children:

The Keane Family Foundation
Mission Statement

The Keane Family Foundation is dedicated to making a difference in a world of many needs. We feel that this can best be done by encouraging role models among young people at risk As a family foundation, we seek to further the values we hold high: respect for oneself and others, belief in individual empowerment, reverence for learning, and faith in the ability to make the world a better place. Our focus is to support programs that can inspire disadvantaged youth to improve their station in life, build their future, and contribute to the betterment of society.

In order to maximize the impact of its resources, the Foundation is limiting grants to youth in the communities in which we live. We are interested in funding organizations, new or established, that will have significant impact through programs that show promise of long-term success. These programs may involve the examination of issues or the implementation of solutions. Through its grants, the Foundation strives to champion children in crisis, nurture integrity and ambition, provide opportunities for enrichment and growth, and promote involvement and performance while building a strong sense of family and community.

This focus has prompted the Keanes to create the Keane Family Scholarship Fund at Harvard College, and in 1993 to help start a non-profit organization called the Project for Young Negotiators. This organization in Charlestown, Massachusetts, teaches negotiation skills as a way to curb violence in the inner city. The Keanes provide seed money, ongoing support, and personal involvement in helping this organization go to scale nationally and internationally. "The joy I get is seeing the impact," says John.

Wealth provides a base of security, adds John, discussing his philosophy of money and the issue of succession in the family foundation. "But after that, it's a tool to reaffirm, nurture, and extend the values that we care about as a family. Our wealth, on the next level, is a vehicle to reach out and to invest in others.

"We have the family members capable of administering and managing the foundation, and keeping alive the values that our family stands for. The problem is not the next two generations, but several generations down the line. I think it's just a matter of time before we, as a family, will have a series of rigorous discussions on the future of the foundation."

- **Carl H. Pforzheimer III.** "My grandfather was a philanthropic person," says Carl H. Pforzheimer III, managing partner of Carl H. Pforzheimer and Co. in New York. Together with his parents and children, Carl has been a member of one of Harvard's most loyal and supportive families:

"My grandfather started our family foundation in 1942 and eventually left a portion of his estate, including his personal library, to it in 1956. A portion of his library was disposed of over the years by the family, bringing in a large infusion to the foundation. Charitable giving is very important, and our foundation can be useful to a society with lots of problems. I come to this belief by way of my father and mother.

"In the early 1990s, my sister and I decided it was time to get the next generation involved in the foundation. We each asked one child to join the board. Her designee has been the same since then, and two of my children rotate onto the board every two to three years. The other is in the Foreign Service and posted abroad much of the time. There are also two outside board members: a business colleague and an educator.

"Our typical minimum gift is $25,000. Our maximum multiyear commitments are generally in the range of $5 million. We meet four times a year, and I talk with the board about how, why, and what we want to give to.

"Our grant making is family-driven, not market-driven, and we operate with a strategy of tiered involvement. Our first priority is to give where foundation trustees and family members are deeply involved—typically on the boards of various nonprofits. There is recognition within the family, and the nonprofits for that matter, that our foundation giving is deliberately linked to personal involvement. Our core giving has been to Harvard, the New York Public Library, and Mount Sinai Hospital, among others.

"The next ring of foundation giving, moving out of the core circle, is 'light' family involvement, and the final tier is supporting causes and issues that we and our friends feel strongly about. We give a great deal to education and scholarship and health care. We don't generally give to 'annual giving,' but rather to specific causes such as Concert Artist Guild, Careers through Culinary Arts, the Dance Theater of Harlem, Pace University, Teach for America, the Henry Street Settlement, Horace Mann School, the Morgan Library, White Plains Hospital, and the South Street Seaport, which lie in this final tier.

"I will remain involved as long as I can. The children will continue to be involved and one of them is likely to emerge as the leader of this family enterprise. We have talked about a spend out, but I see no reason to do so. It is my hope that the foundation continues into my grandchildren's generation and beyond. It is great fun, is good for our family, and is helpful to society."

- **Andrea Okamura.** "I love sports, and joined the Harvard tennis team as a walk-on in my junior year," says Andi Okamura of Atherton, California, explaining the genesis of the gift she and her husband, Jeff Chambers, donated to Harvard. In 1999, they made a substantial commitment to the College for women's athletics. "I learned a lot about myself playing on the team—about my willingness to take risks and how I deal with winning and losing. It was a great experience for me. I am a big believer in athletics for everyone, and my gift will enhance women's participation at the College."

Besides playing tennis at Harvard, Andi sang in the Collegium Musicum, took voice lessons, and eventually completed an MFA in music performance at Boston University. Today, she is an active volunteer for a number of Bay Area institutions, including the schools attended by her two sons, Sacred Heart and St. Joseph's. She is also on the board of the East Palo Alto Tennis and Tutorial program and runs its annual fundraising dinner.

"We teach tennis and arrange for academic tutoring for underprivileged kids in East Palo Alto. The program has been very successful in giving them a sense of accomplishment and an experience in teamwork. I've followed a number of kids in the program, and some have gone on to great things. It's part of our community, part of our lives, and I love that.

"Jeff and I give to Harvard, Winsor, East Side Prep, Sacred Heart, St. Joseph's, San Francisco Opera, the Boys and Girls Club in San Francisco, and a number of health-related causes. Our focus is on education and children, but we give to a broad array of organizations. It's very rewarding."

Andi and Jeff plan to expand their giving. "There is an amount of money, beyond what we need and will give to our children, that we can give away," she adds. "It's satisfying to make a difference, and I feel good helping to improve the lives of others. I want to involve our sons—sooner rather than later—in our family philanthropy to let them discover the joy in giving."

■ **Gregory C. Carr.** "I care deeply about human rights, the environment, and the arts, and that is where I am going to make a difference," says Greg Carr, discussing his philanthropy. "It's great fun to be passionate about these areas and make something happen."

Greg has a history of making things happen. He cofounded Boston Technology, Inc., in 1986 and eventually became chairman of the global Internet service provider Prodigy, Inc. In 1999, he sold a portion of his interest in Prodigy and formed his own private family foundation. He also made an $18 million gift to the John F. Kennedy School of Government at Harvard to create the Carr Center for Human Rights Policy.

"Human rights is a discipline that needs to be professionalized, and the Carr Center will help bring intellectual rigor to this issue," he says. "I see Harvard assisting human rights organizations around the world with research, teaching, and training on the best practices. I've been able to bring Harvard to my home state of Idaho, where the Kennedy School is training local officials on how best to promote human rights."

Greg is also expanding the scope of the natural history museum in Idaho Falls and donated the funds for the construction of a recently completed theater, Zero Arrow Street, in Cambridge. In addition, he serves on the board of Physicians for Human Rights.

Greg says that managing his foundation is his full-time job. "I enjoy this activity and am using professional skills from my for-profit life to think about what I can achieve philanthropically," he adds. "I spent time thinking about the name of the foundation and decided on a *family* name. The Carr Foundation is for all of my family to work on and be proud of. We are making a statement about what we care about."

Conclusion

Clearly, there are a variety of ways to organize and approach your individual and family philanthropy. The rewards of the effort can be deeply satisfying: making the world a better place and strengthening your family.

In the case of my family, we recently held a meeting of my generation (eight of us, including spouses) to discuss a family gift from my father's donor advised fund. After a debate on the issues of focus and purpose and a subsequent site visit, we settled on one grant to the Kidney Foundation of Massachusetts, since two people in our immediate family have had kidney transplants.

I learned more about my sisters as they talked about what was important to them. This was a bonus that I had hoped for, and my family's experience illustrates the continuing value of engaging in family philanthropy.

CHAPTER 9

Family Meetings

Families meet informally all the time. That is how family members communicate and share their lives. Families that need to make decisions together—especially families of wealth—can also benefit from more formal meetings. Meetings of this kind help to build effective families. Formal family meetings allow nuclear or multigenerational families to meet in a more structured, and therefore safer, environment. The purpose is to share information, learn about one another, make joint decisions, understand the family's financial wealth, discuss ways to give back to society, begin or perpetuate family traditions, discuss leadership issues, and forge or preserve the family's vision for the future. Meetings enable the next generation to participate in the family business or the business of the family. In short, these gatherings provide families with a forum to discuss and enhance not only financial capital but also "relational capital," strengthening the system of family relationships across generations.

Family meetings begin the joint decision-making process for the family members, leading to a more formal governance structure. Governance centers on the following question: how are we, as a family, going to organize ourselves to solve financial and personal issues, make joint decisions, and plan for the future? (See Chapter 5 for more about family governance.)

In addition to creating such a decision-making process, two themes are key to successful family meetings. First is the appreciation of "differentness." Because these meetings require the coming together of different family members, participants soon discover that each person is a unique individual pursuing their own identities. A family can thrive only if it permits differentness to be recognized and honored. Meetings allowing for the rigorous discussion of differences before a decision is made will lead to a greater degree of satisfaction for the individuals and the group. Appreciating differences can be a source of discomfort if it is not understood as part of good family meeting dialogue. With that in mind, a family meeting becomes an opportunity for family members to define themselves around the topics and issues that are discussed as components of the agenda.

Families should also bear in mind that life is all about transitions. Births, deaths, marriages, divorces, relocations, sending children to college, retirement, and succession planning for the family enterprise or philanthropy are common changes to be managed. Dealing with the allocation of substantial wealth is also a transition that can increase the pressure on some family members and ultimately may impair their thinking. A family meeting marks life's changes and helps family members manage themselves in life's transitional moments, including sharing information about the family's financial wealth. For example, bringing younger family members into the meeting (beginning around age 10) or formally including young adults in the work of family philanthropy are transitions that can be used as rites of passage initiating the next generation into the family's sacred information and its work. A family meeting is an opportunity for the next generation to gain new knowledge and become a stakeholder.

The Stories

Jay Hughes sees many family meetings that begin with "what" and "how" questions: What asset classes should we invest in with the proceeds from our liquidity event? How should we leverage the generation-skipping tax exclusion? The main part of the meeting's agenda is often designed by advisers and is based on a financial transaction or new estate planning maneuver. He suggests that families adopt a different perspective.

"I have learned two key facts about successful family meetings," says Hughes. "First, the initial meeting should be qualitative and not quantitative. The agenda should stress the 'why' and 'what if' questions: Why should we work together? What if we included our sons and daughters-in-law in our family philanthropy? The core issues that a family ought to address early on should focus on the human and intellectual capital of the family.

"Second, in one of the earliest family meetings, more than a third of the time should be devoted to storytelling. Ask the elders to tell the family's most important stories. Stories help families understand the past so that they can envision the future."

Family stories are vital to the well-being of a family and need to be told time and again. They provide a view of the family's history and send a message to the children, in-laws, and grandchildren that they belong and that their family is unique. The next generation gains a sense of the vital "differentness" of their family. Moreover, one reason for the proverb "shirtsleeves-to-shirtsleeves in three generations" being true is that the individuals in the third and fourth generations often have no connection to the source of the family's financial wealth. They have no idea what it took to create the money they must now steward. Family stories keep that connection alive for many generations. One family that emphasizes its stories is the Cabots of Boston.

"The family stories are so important to us that we have an archives committee and a family newsletter," says Edmund "Ned" Cabot, M.D., discussing the various committees of his multigenerational family organization, the Godfrey Lowell Cabot Family Association. One branch of the Cabots, with more than 100 members, has established committees on the archives, the family newsletter, philanthropy, events, financial education, company shareholders, and the nominating process. All of these committees report to the 10-member Family Council. Every few years, the archives committee puts out a CD on the family history.

"Our family meeting is a form of networking," says Cabot. "It's a way to keep extended family members who are spread all around the country and the world closer together than they otherwise would be. The annual meeting's outcome is that we share information of mutual interest such as philanthropy, the Cabot Corporation, and our ancestral heritage.

"A lot of storytelling goes on in my family at our ranch in Colorado," Cabot adds. "The stories are about my parents, what my father achieved, and what life was like for him. All families would benefit from a tradition in which the elders tell such stories to the grandchildren."

The Agenda

The agenda functions as the centerpiece of effective family meetings, shaping the opportunity for deep learning to occur. You may want to cover numerous topics during your family meetings, including preparing the next generation for a financial inheritance, being a resource for children's and cousins' career development, making decisions about grants as a part of the family's philanthropy, designing a family website, discussing a new estate planning strategy, or reporting on investment results. All of these ideas, and many more, can be positioned within an overarching agenda marked by four headings: *human capital, intellectual capital, social capital,* and *financial capital.* This master agenda gives participants the big picture and balances the emphases across the broader philosophical purposes of family meetings.

I worked with Bill and Gayle Chorske to design an agenda for their family meeting in Florida with their adult children, their children's spouses, a niece, and a nephew. Here is their agenda:

Chorske Family meeting

Human Capital

- Chorske family history

- How do we define "family"?

- What does this family want to preserve besides our financial wealth?

Intellectual Capital

- What challenges do the 10 of you see as you think about working together?

- How do we foster leadership in the next generation?

Social Capital

- How do we make our foundation more effective?

- How do we increase the second generation's involvement?

- What are the next steps?

- Update on the Chorske Family Scholarship at the University of Minnesota

Financial Capital

- Funding the grandchildren's education

"Turning seventy was a big event for me," says Bill Chorske, speaking about his family meeting with his three children, a niece and nephew, and all their spouses. "It was time to talk with my children about the future and encourage them to pick up the family leadership and increase their involvement in the family foundation. In fact, Gayle and I asked who could take a leadership role in our foundation at this time, and my daughter, younger son, and niece volunteered to do the work.

"It was important to me that we used this opportunity to tell our children that my niece and nephew [children of his deceased brother] and their spouses should now be seen as full members of our family. They will have equal access to the family's philanthropy and ultimately to its financial wealth. This was a powerful conversation and a moving moment for all of us."

Bill says that he and Gayle planned to have separate follow-up meetings with their children and their spouses to tell them about their inheritances and discuss what it means to them.

"Organizing the agenda of our family meeting around the four capitals worked well," adds Bill, describing his use of the human, intellectual, social and financial capital to organize the day. "The concept of the four capitals gave us the framework to think about our family and the topics we need to deal with now and in the future."

Kathy Wiseman, founder and president of Working Systems, a Washington, D. C., consulting firm, is dedicated to helping families, their foundations, firms, and family offices manage transitions effectively. She agrees that planning a meeting agenda around the broad topics of the family's human, intellectual, social, and financial capital is evolving into a best practice. Indeed, she suggests that early on a family ought to ask themselves: What is our vision for the human, the intellectual, the social, and the financial capital of our family? I asked Kathy to elaborate on this strategy and other ideas that she thinks are critical to successful family meetings.

COLLIER: What is a family meeting's primary purpose?

WISEMAN: To encourage that family's members to work together and make decisions in a structured way. A family holds a "family meeting" to plan for the future, share information so that the plan they produce is coherent and durable, and determine who in the family will take responsibility for the family's financial assets.

COLLIER: What is the difference between a family meeting and a family reunion?

WISEMAN: I see a family reunion as a social event for many branches of a family. A family meeting may also include several branches but the focus is on a topic where information-sharing and joint decision-making are necessary—between parents and the next generation. A family meeting has an agreed-on outcome, and those outcomes typically call for financial education, decision-making, communication, and the building of consensus.

COLLIER: What goals do families typically want to achieve?

WISEMAN: Many family members know they need to make decisions together and that inexperience could lead to conflict. Holding a family meeting is a way to air differences and build toward agreement in an organized and productive manner—with any luck, giving rise to new skills within the family.

It always helps to make the meeting's purpose clear from the outset. Is the purpose to share information? Is it to prepare the family for a decision they need to make soon? Is it a chance for people to get to know one another better or to discuss family governance? Everyone deserves to have a feel for the purpose—before the meeting starts.

COLLIER: Can you elaborate on the various purposes for family meetings?

WISEMAN: I see a great deal of variation surrounding the purposes. A purpose could be to plan a parents' anniversary event, set rules for how the summer house will be managed, provide information about investments, talk about the financial inheritance, engage in family philanthropy, or decide who will be the trustees of the family trusts. When families hold meetings to share such information before the wealth-creator dies, the next generation can understand the thinking behind those decisions.

COLLIER: When should the children or grandchildren be included in family meetings?

WISEMAN: Personally, I would include children age 10 and above in some part of the family meeting. They may not be involved in the decision-making, but they'll hear the information exchange about the business of the family. Doing so conveys the idea that "a family meeting is something we believe in, and we want you to be a good contributor—therefore we are going to expose you to the meeting atmosphere at a young age."

COLLIER: Should parents involve their adult children in planning the agenda?

WISEMAN: It's no surprise that family members do better if they have a say in the agenda. Giving participants a stake in the design raises their level of commitment and the overall quality of participation. Some family leaders disagree. They say: "You know, it's our meeting. It's our agenda. We're going to do what we want." However, planning an effective agenda takes time and thought and can be a capacity-builder for the next generation.

COLLIER: Who should be invited to attend the family meeting?

WISEMAN: That's a difficult question. Here's a principle you can start with: Anyone who is, or who will be, affected by the decisions being made at the meeting should be included.

You could start with one group—immediate family, for example—and then later on include spouses, partners, and in-laws. Some families have difficulty deciding whether to include the in-laws. This decision should be based on a set of criteria and the result should be communicated to all interested parties. Regardless of whom you decide to include, you should communicate the criteria to each family member. This one action goes a long way toward improving family relationships and diminishing feelings of exclusion.

COLLIER: How often should a family hold family meetings?

WISEMAN: It depends on what has to get done. If a family has an active business enterprise or philanthropy, more meetings are often required. For example, they could meet several times a year, with smaller committee meetings throughout the year. For families that are just beginning to work together and do not have to make immediate decisions, I recommend meeting twice a year for the first two years, and then once a year.

COLLIER: What agenda items should a family discuss other than its financial wealth?

WISEMAN: The best topics are those that are relevant to the family in two ways. First, whatever is important now. And second, what will be important in 10 years. Many families organize their meetings around the "four capitals"—human, intellectual, social, and financial. Some of my favorite topics concern understanding the wealth's origin and the sacrifices that have been made to acquire it. Additional topics include: encouraging each family member's pursuit of their passion; designing an appropriate form of governance; conducting a thoughtful philanthropic strategy; preparing the next generation to be competent stewards of the family money; and discussing the challenges that are facing the family in the future.

COLLIER: How should a family begin their family meetings?

WISEMAN: I begin my meetings with a set of "catching up" questions that everyone is encouraged to answer, such as:

- What did you learn this past year from either an accomplishment or a challenge?

- What is an interesting, novel way in which you differ from others in the family? How are you the same?

- What is your most important passion?

This opening exercise allows family members to relate to one another. Note how these aren't the kinds of thing you hear, or heard, around the dining room table. Catching up is important and too many families skip over this piece because they think they know one another well. In some ways, these questions go beyond catching up. The "passion" question in particular is a good example.

COLLIER: What are the main challenges you see in family meetings?

WISEMAN: I see three key challenges. One is negotiating a succession plan for the family money and the family philanthropy. Another is geographical dispersion—ways to get around those physical distances—and maintain participation. Finally comes family "differentness"—which can turn out to be the most critical.

In a family, individuals differ in skills and abilities, points of view, and life experiences. For years, over many interactions, family members have responded to these differences in reactive ways. Because many families are uncomfortable with members who are different, they can be overly sensitive. The biggest challenge in a family meeting is to manage the reactivity and reduce the programmed responses.

Some participants assume that everyone in the family should be the same, believing that this would make life easier. Well, maybe it can make the first part of the meeting easier. Even so, it will become clear that we are different—and it's a difficult process to allow participants to feel good about how they are different. Differences are a source of vitality. Yet certain differences can cause meetings to go off track.

COLLIER: So what should be done, early on, about that risk?

WISEMAN: In the beginning, someone has to keep repeating: "This is a chance for us to learn more about one another, to learn about our differences and how we may work together." That's a critical piece of the process, and a key element for any facilitator.

COLLIER: What are the typical outcomes of family meetings?

WISEMAN: The most valuable meetings are those where participants acquire an experience of one another that differs from whatever they brought to the event. The meeting may or may not achieve its purpose. Even if it doesn't, participants can feel that they have learned something about one another and are now able to respect the individual differences of family members.

Now and then, a meeting can change the very nature of the family, because meetings allow people to discuss critical issues, manage the differences, and survive. I've seen it happen. Not enough, but it does happen. And for those who have the experience, it's profound and moving. One family member said to me: "Being together and working with my family was something I dreaded. After participating in the family meetings, I am amazed at the genuineness of the experience—and how clear I am about my family's importance to me."

COLLIER: What is a family diagram? Why would that be an important topic for an early family meeting?

WISEMAN: A family diagram is a large "picture" of one's family—the people, the pertinent events of their lives, and the family relationships over time. When it's done right, the diagram represents a large quantity of data that describes the history of the family and its relationship component. The diagram can be the basis for a meeting discussion. Such a tool offers an opportunity to gather new facts and learn—partly by seeing—the family's history from differing perspectives. [For more information on family diagrams, see *Extraordinary Relationships* and *You Can Go Home Again: Reconnecting with Your Family* as listed in the bibliography.]

Despite a family's differences and all the varying perspectives, the result of gathering family information reinforces a simple truth: "You are a member of this complex family, and the diagram provides information to describe it"—bringing the whole landscape into the light. My experience is that a family that creates such a diagram gains insights that allow them to have deeper and more meaningful conversations and make more informed choices about the future.

COLLIER: Can a family meeting prepare the next generation?

WISEMAN: Most definitely. Family meetings can help parents prepare their children and grandchildren to take responsibility for the family wealth, family philanthropy, and maintaining open family relationships. Over time, family meetings prepare families to work together, make complicated decisions, and maintain a network of relationships that can act as a resource for one another across the generations. While family meetings take a great deal of time and work, the benefits can make a significant difference for the family, its ability to work together, and its vision for the future.

Epilogue

In the long run the possessor of great wealth is judged in part by the use he makes of his riches, including in that use his disposal of them at his death.

CHARLES W. ELIOT AB 1853
President of Harvard University, 1869–1909
from *Great Riches* (1906)

I began this book with a series of questions and will end in the same way. What do you and your family *really* value? How can you help to guide your children's life journey? What kind of vision does your family aspire to achieve?

My message is a simple one: The real wealth of your family is not financial. Because of this, your individual principles and family's vision should be discussed *before* implementing various estate planning strategies. Moreover, you can keep your family's human capital growing over time by thinking periodically about your role and your family's role in promoting each family member's growth and development.

A personal mission statement, an ethical will, or a philosophy of life is a statement to your children of the kind of legacy you want to leave them and how you want to be remembered. Defining a vision for the future is a family exercise others are using. The conversation, the planning, and the journey with your children are what matter most. John O'Neill, a business leadership consultant, says it well in his book *Leadership Aikido*: "A plan is nothing more than a road map to a destination that will leave you changed—a different person from the one that started the trip."

Defining the most important themes surrounding family wealth is something the late Reverend Professor Peter J. Gomes thought about in fresh ways. "My thesis involves the distinction between 'making a living' and 'making a life,'" said Gomes, then Plummer Professor of Christian Morals and Pusey Minister in The Memorial Church at Harvard University. "What it means to make a life is difficult to articulate because we are still uneasy talking about money. The problems are: Who gets the money? Do you really know what to do with it? How do you talk about it? There is a conspiracy of silence today, and little serious discourse on the social and moral uses of wealth."

Gomes made the case for communication concerning our financial wealth and reminded us of the complex place of money in the American landscape, as described by Daphne Merkin in a *New Yorker* article: "Although my family's now-you-see-it, now-you-don't approach to money may have been particularly heated, I slowly came to realize that this private obfuscation was embedded within a larger cultural evasiveness. I noticed that other people were caught in a similarly ambivalent grip. No one was honest about the subject of money; worse yet, not many people seemed to recognize that they were dishonest. People either deified money or demonized it."

Wealth looms large in our society today and is a highly charged part of our lives. It has the power to "create capacity"—to help individuals discover and pursue their calling. But it can also subvert that effort. "Money has profound meaning in our society," says columnist Esther M. Berger in a *Town and Country* article. "It has become a metaphor for many things, some positive (freedom and philanthropy, for example) and some decidedly negative (condescension and control)."

In short, we need to be "awake" to the messages surrounding money that we send to our children and aware of those messages we inherited from our own parents. As Gomes pointed out, "We need to raise our consciousness about our wealth and the effect of the choices we make."

Thus, the important choices we make about our financial wealth are linked to what we value and are often driven by a strong sense of urgency. These decisions matter on a deeper level because of our own impending death. But the fact that we are going to die can set us free. "The more we refuse to look at our own death, the more we repress and deny new possibilities for living," says the Rev. Alan W. Jones, former dean of Grace Cathedral in San Francisco, in his book, *Soul Making*. "We are all going to die, and our life is a movement to that sure end . . . . Meditation on this simple fact has a wonderful way of clearing the mind! It enables us to live every single moment with new appreciation and delight. The willingness to live with the knowledge of our inevitable death enables us to face, more and more, both the freedom and responsibility that life offers . . . . As Don Juan reminds Castaneda: 'In a world where death is a hunter, . . . there is no time for regrets or doubts. There is only time for decisions.'"

Who am I, then, in light of my own mortality? This question leads us to reflect on our legacy—the extension of our life that continues after death. What kind of legacy do we want to leave—to our families, to our society, to the world at large?

Philanthropy has the potential to inspire a personal legacy and allow us to leave a lasting mark. In his book, *The Age of Paradox*, Charles Handy, business consultant and fellow of the London Business School, reflects on the meaning of legacy. Handy writes, "It is a search for a cause. The cause, however, to be truly satisfying must be a 'purpose beyond oneself,' because to be turned in on oneself, said St. Augustine, is the greatest of sins; because we discover ourselves through others, said Jung; because the immortality, for which we all privately long, is really immortality through others."

"Philanthropy is a way for mortals to pursue immortality," concluded Peter Gomes:

> Wealth is not just private treasure for private use. Money has civic content and society has a claim on our money. The wisdom of "to whom much is given, much is expected" has had a firm place in the moral landscape of the West for thousands of years.
>
> This is not a new mandate, but it is being redefined today. How do I strike a balance between what is good for me and my family, and what is good for society? Building family and building society go together. Money is a means to an end, morally neutral but with public consequences.
>
> How do you want to be remembered? How do you wish history to record you? What lasting imprint do you want to leave on the world? Thinking through what your life is evolving toward is the central task in "making a life." Enjoy what you have by sorting out what to leave. Legacy ought to be a life's work.

A "Family Systems" Approach to the Estate Planning Process*

While meeting with your clients, Bill and Ann, you learn that Ann is upset that their first son Tom and his wife, Kate, have been less communicative since their first child was born. Moreover, their daughter-in-law says she will not invite them to Thanksgiving dinner for the foreseeable future. In response to this change, Ann wants to fund Tom's inheritance through a restrictive trust and at a level lesser than their younger son.

As their attorney you listen to their comments and want to carry out their wishes. However, you know that something is changing in the family, and while you may not know it, you are now part of an emotional triangle in this family system: Bill/Ann—Tom—you. This new triangle may reduce Ann's anxiety, but it inadvertently encourages Bill and Ann to ignore the real problem, the underlying relational issues with their son, and to make an important estate planning decision based more on emotion than on careful thought. How might you help them think differently about an anxiety-driven decision? What could you say? How should you think about your role in the triangle?

Answers to these questions may lie in a psychological framework that informs how we might think differently about estate planning: family systems theory. Family systems theory, developed initially by Dr. Murray Bowen in the 1950s, describes the emotional functioning of families. It focuses more on family interactions than on structure, more on relationships than on individuals, and more on the whole than on the parts. Family systems theory provides clues to understanding how our most important relationships affect our functioning and our life course.

Viewing our clients through the family systems lens can contribute to our ability to help them be a bit more thoughtful and effective in the decisions they make about their estate plan. Let me be clear: this is not a form of psy-

---

*This article appeared in the ACTEC (The American College of Trust and Estate Counsel) Journal in 2004.

chotherapy, nor am I suggesting that you become an expert in family systems theory. I am simply suggesting that you can 1) deepen your understanding about a family's emotional process, 2) provide a different presence for your families, and 3) ask a set of questions that are more subtle and nuanced. "Asking questions," says the late Dr. Edwin H. Friedman, a family systems specialist, in his book, *Generation to Generation*, "is a great way to remain both nonanxious and present."

The highest and best purpose of the estate planning process is, for me, to facilitate the effective transfer of an appropriate amount of financial assets to succeeding generations of family members in a way that will improve their life course. Families that are effective in this process exhibit a number of common qualities. They treat their adult children with respect, openness, and clear communication. They strive to work with them as equals. The family money provides freedom and flexibility for their children, but is not so important as to be key to their sense of self worth. They use considered principles to guide their decision-making surrounding the uses of the family money. Foremost among the guiding principles is the assumption that adult children should take responsibility for their lives.

Moreover, they ask their children (and more often than not their children's spouses) essential questions about their life course and the purpose of a financial inheritance. They ask questions like:

- "What are your passions in life and how can we invest in them?"

- "What are your most important values and principles?"

- "How would you think about the purposes a financial inheritance might serve in your life?"

- "How much money do you need from us to live a worthwhile life?"

- "What allocation do you think would be best for you: how much outright, how much in trust, and/or how much in a philanthropic fund?"

Before I give you my best thinking on how the family systems model may improve the estate planning process and what new questions you may want to ask your clients, let me provide a brief introduction to Bowen theory and two of its concepts.

First, think of the family system as a mobile, where family members react to each other as parts of the mobile as it tilts and sways. The behavior or emotions of one person can often trigger an anxious reaction in other members of the family, i.e., the system. The nuclear family is an emotional unit and each of us is only a fragment of a bigger unit. We are governed by emotional forces in our families and our responses to them.

"Bowen family systems theory postulates that the basic emotional functioning of each human individual is defined in the crucible of the relationship of an individual and his primary caretakers and is an outcome of a multigenerational process," writes Kathy K. Wiseman, MBA, a family business consultant in Washington, D.C., and editor of *The Emotional Side of Organizations*. "People are born into families and develop patterns of responding to significant relationships and events. These ways of responding remain pretty much intact even when they become adults." All of us have some degree of anxiety in our relationships. This anxiety is a result of complex attachments to parents that are managed in predictable ways. Too much closeness without independent thinking or cutoff can be observed when sensitivity gets too great. Cutoff is one way that individuals manage their unresolved emotional issues with their family members by reducing contact with them. All families manage anxiety in predictable ways, including triangles.

Triangles

Often, the anxiety within family relationships can be so intense and uncomfortable that an individual will automatically "triangle" in a third person to reduce the stress. Triangles are a key concept in the family systems model and constitute a primary pattern of behavior in families. Triangles are not good or bad; they "just are." In fact, families can have a number of overlapping triangles in play at the same time. There are, for example, triangles between Bill—Ann—Tom, Bill—Ann—daughter-in-law, Bill—Ann—attorney.

For example, your client could triangle in their son or daughter-in-law or the family money, or you, the family attorney. Their conversations with you may reduce their anxiety and help to manage the conflict in their life without dealing with the issue at hand: a marital dispute, the son's behavior, the daughter-in-law's differences or the terms of a restrictive trust.

"Emotional triangles are the building blocks of any relationship system," says Friedman in his book, *A Failure of Nerve*. "Emotional triangles thus have both negative and positive effects…their negative aspect is that they perpetuate treadmills, they reduce clarity in thinking processes, they distort perceptions, they inhibit decisiveness, and they transmit stress."

Triangles serve a function by reducing the anxiety in important relationships. A husband and wife cannot resolve serious personal issues, so the husband triangles in work or an affair. A daughter has continuing heated disagreements with her mother and triangles in her father, covertly seeking to pressure her father to intervene on her behalf. Although triangles fulfill a function, the pattern can be unhealthy. It is, however, possible to be "triangle savvy" if one of the three individuals can see their part in the family drama, and take responsibility for themselves.

Differentiation

Differentiation is one of eight major concepts in family systems theory. It describes one's ability, over a lifetime, to strive to be a little better at 1) thinking for one's self and taking a principled stand on issues, 2) making thoughtful decisions based more on facts than on emotions, and 3) being less anxious and reactive in the face of intense family emotionality or resistance.

This is hard to accomplish. Because of the emotion inherent in any family system, most people who are exposed to Bowen theory and are able to work on "self" can, over a lifetime, only improve their effectiveness a little bit. Of course, we have a say in how we act and what kind of presence we present to others, but our cellular makeup from multigenerational emotional processes determines our predisposition around reactivity and sensitivity to others.

Differentiation is not the same as maturity, individuation, or emotional intelligence, but these ideas, in my view, are part of differentiation. Less differentiated or less mature families inhibit the individuation that allows family members to gain perspective and to separate in healthy ways.

Dr. Friedman sums up differentiation well: "I want to stress that by well-differentiated...I do not mean someone who autocratically tells others what to do or coercively orders them around, although any leader who defines him or herself clearly may be perceived that way by those who are not taking responsibility for their own emotional being and destiny. Rather, I mean someone who has clarity about his or her own life goals, and, therefore, someone who is less likely to become lost in the anxious emotional processes swirling about. I mean someone who can be separate while still remaining connected, and therefore can maintain a modifying, non-anxious, and sometimes challenging presence. I mean someone who can manage his or her own reactivity to the automatic reactivity of others, and therefore be able to take stands at the risk of displeasing."

The family systems model suggests to me new ways of thinking about the estate planning process. A family's estate planning and the final distribution of their financial assets is one, among many, of the important events and processes in the life cycle. In fact, it can be thought of as a major life transition, indeed a rite of passage that the children—not just the parents—go through.

"When family systems concepts are applied to such nodal events," writes Friedman in *Generation to Generation*, "it becomes clear that, far from being an intermediary, it is the family itself that is going through the passage, rather than only some 'identified' celebrant(s), and the family may actually go through more changes than the focused member(s)."

Since your client's adult children will be deeply affected by these important financial and family decisions, it becomes an opportunity to involve the entire family and prepare them—financially and emotionally—for this life transition.

Involving the family means more than simply telling them the full financial situation and complete story of the family; it means asking for their input. Including adult children, at an age-appropriate time, encourages them to take responsibility for their financial inheritance and indeed for their entire financial life.

Ann D. Bunting, PhD, a psychologist and founder of the Vermont Center for Family Studies in Burlington, recently published an article describing a fair and objective way for distributing the possessions of an estate. Her article, "Estate Planning and Family Relationships: A Commentary on an Estate Distribution Method," appears in the 2003 issue of the journal *Family Systems*.

I asked Dr. Bunting how she would think about applying the tenets of family systems theory to the estate planning process. She said, "Parents need to be clear themselves—individually and as a couple—about what principles will guide their decisions about the estate allocation. Then they can have an open and respectful conversation with their children, saying in effect, this is what we are thinking based on the principles we believe, and we want your ideas, although we will make the ultimate decision." These principles might include not giving them the entire estate, taking into account individual differences, standing for the value of meaningful work, and providing a portion for philanthropy.

In working with families of wealth, Bunting has seen how hard this is for couples to accomplish, in part because they have typically never had a discussion with the children about the impact of money on the family. "Moreover, parents are afraid about their reactivity to the children's response and the children's reactivity to them," she says. "It is all about the differentiation of the parents and their ability to take a thoughtful and principled stand on the estate distribution before they talk to their children."

Kathy Wiseman agrees and adds, "Engaging adult children in a dialogue begins a process that can make a difference for the family in the future.

Asking their opinion makes sense. I do not think parents are asking them to make the ultimate decision, but they are asking for more information, and in doing that, the parents can make a decision based on the facts their children contribute. It is a more knowledge-based decision rather than one based on speculation, emotion, and a fear of losing control."

Including adult children in the financial allocation decision process may foster self-responsibility. It could also be a way for families to work together, work out family relationship issues in healthy ways, and think about what is important. What does the money stand for: freedom, philanthropy, or life-style maintenance? An ongoing discussion can be a form of preparation for taking responsibility for the financial inheritance.

"When there is wealth to be managed," adds Wiseman, "it takes practice. Sooner or later, some children are going to work together, so using the estate planning process while the parents are alive has enormous benefit."

When children take responsibility for themselves, individual differences are valued. "There is a tendency in families to reach for consensus and, in that process, dampen individual difference," says Wiseman. She suggests that estate planning is best thought of as both an individual and family process. "An open discussion allows for differences to emerge, and that fosters a broader inclusiveness. We do not all need to be the same to reach a decision that serves us as a group. This process may give parents permission to leave different amounts to their children because the decision is not arbitrary but based on informed inequality."

I have discovered that couples are eager to discuss a set of questions that focus on family in addition to the financial arrangements. These are questions our client families rarely have the opportunity to ask and answer in the context of family—their most important relationships. Here are six questions you may want to use with your wealthy clients.

- What principles guide your thinking about what is an appropriate inheritance for your children?

- What amount of money would be life-enhancing?

- When has money worked well in your family?

- Could you give your children a say in their financial inheritance?

- What will your children think if they do not have to work?

- How do you (and your children) think about the ultimate division between your family's private wealth and public philanthropy?

Let me summarize five key ideas from family systems thinking that may be useful to you in your estate planning work:

- There are multi-generational emotional forces at work in your client families. Take a broader view of each family's functioning.

- Anxiety and emotional reactivity are present in all families to some degree.

- Individuals use triangles to manage anxiety in the family system. They may well triangle in the family advisor.

- Children who are portrayed as the "black sheep" are often using emotional or geographic cutoff to manage the anxiety in their relationship to their parents. The parents play a role in their children's cutoff process.

- The goal is to work on differentiation, that is, for each family member to be able to take a principled stand, "hang in there," and stay connected to the family.

My summary of how you may want to use the family systems approach in your work is as follows:

- Be a calm, non-reactive presence whenever you meet with clients.

- Observe your role in the triangle and think about whether you are taking sides between spouses or between parents and their adult children.

- Focus on the strengths in the family—i.e., those family members with the greatest capacity for change and self-definition.

- Keep in mind the broader perspective of the family's emotional history. What are some of the important events in the family's history that influence their thinking or behavior?

- Support your clients in encouraging their children to lead their own lives.

- Promote individuality and family members taking responsibility for themselves, their financial situation, and their life course.

- Include adult children in the decisions surrounding their financial inheritance.

- Ask probing questions surrounding the impact of the financial inheritance on family members: "What will be the effect of this money on your children?"

Family systems theory makes a serious contribution to the estate planning process. It emphasizes responsibility for self while staying connected to the family and has clear application to your work as an attorney: promoting responsibility around the family money through inclusiveness in the next generation.

If we can see more clearly each client's role in the family's drama, ask penetrating questions, and challenge them to self-reflection, this process might well help them make more thoughtful and effective estate planning decisions.

Family Questionnaire #1

These questions are designed to help you begin thinking about your wealth, your philanthropy, and the future of your family.

Your Principles

1. Which of the following are most important to you? (Please rank each of these from 1 to 5, with 1 as the highest and 5 as the lowest value.)

Personal achievement	_____	Hard work	_____
Career success	_____	Self-esteem	_____
Financial independence	_____	Service to others	_____
Family unity and tradition	_____	Permanent legacy	_____
Responsible uses of money	_____	Philanthropy	_____
Creativity	_____	Volunteerism	_____
Spirituality	_____	Community standing	_____
		Other	_____

2. Who or what was the greatest influence on you in developing your principles?

Parents	_____	Mentors	_____
Other relatives	_____	Personal experiences	_____
Teachers	_____	Other	_____

3. How did your family achieve their present financial status?

Inherited wealth	_____	Personal effort	_____
Good fortune	_____	Support from others	_____

4. Describe your parents' and grandparents' financial histories.

_____

_____

5. Which financial decisions made by your parents continue to affect you the most today?

_____

_____

6. How much money do you need to spend each year to live comfortably?

_____

_____

Your Children

1. What principles seem to guide your children's lives?

_____

_____

When you consider your grandchildren, what principles would you like to communicate to them?

_____

_____

2. How wealthy do you want your children (and grandchildren) to become?

Age	Capital	Income
20s	_____	_____
30s	_____	_____
40s	_____	_____

What purposes do you think they want the money to serve?

_____

3. What are the pros and cons of leaving substantial wealth to your children?

Pros:

_____

Cons:

_____

4. How will you know that your children have the judgment and skills to use inherited wealth constructively?

_____

_____

5. In what ways do you hope your children will be philanthropic?

_____

_____

6. What is your experience of working together in your family?

_____

_____

Your Philanthropy

1. How does your charitable giving represent what is important to you and/or your family?

_____

_____

2. What institutions, organizations, and people have been most important to you in your life?

_____

_____

3. What values do you hope that money will promote in your family?

_____

_____

4. There are three basic beneficiaries of your estate: your heirs, institutions and causes that matter to you, and the IRS.

What is the current percentage distribution?

Heirs_____%   Philanthropy_____%   IRS_____%

What would you like it to be?

Heirs_____%   Philanthropy_____%   IRS_____%

5. Are you aware of some methods that can be used to modify these percentages to resemble your goals more closely?

Yes: _____   No: _____

Family Questionnaire #2
(The Philanthropic Initiative)

1. Considering our history as a family, do we understand and agree on our core family values? How would you express them?

   _____

   _____

2. Do your values differ from those in your family? If so, how would you express that difference?

   _____

   _____

3. The family is fortunate to have significant resources that can be used to enable its members to further important personal business and philanthropic interests. What is your view of these resources, and what opportunities, risks, and issues do they represent to you?

   _____

   _____

4. Does a family foundation seem like a good idea? If so, why? If not, why not?

   _____

   _____

   How do you think a family foundation should be organized?

   _____

   _____

5. Individually, we have a history of charitable giving and volunteerism. Do we know why we made those gifts of money and time? Do we feel good about our choices? Do we know if our efforts made any difference?

_____

_____

   a. Which of our past gifts have given us the most satisfaction?

   _____

   _____

   b. Which have given us the least?

   _____

   _____

6. What criteria would you, as a donor, and perhaps as a trustee of a family foundation, put on proposals before they were funded?

_____

_____

7. Considering the future, what are the things about which you feel passionate? What are the things that really interest you? There are many major issues facing society, including the arts, children's causes, civil rights, education, environment, housing, and abolishing hunger. They are all important, but which ones would you give the highest priority? Which ones do you feel are most important and why?

_____

_____

8. To what extent would you like to be involved in the work of exploring and/or analyzing problems and shaping promising solutions?

_____

_____

9. To develop a process that works for each of us, what steps would be the most helpful for you to learn about the things that interest you?

    Research on specific subjects   _____
    Site visits to nonprofit organizations   _____
    Background information to read   _____
    Visits with experts   _____

10. How much direct contact with donees would you like to have?

    _____

    _____

11. Given your other commitments, how much time do you have to devote to philanthropy?

    _____

    _____

12. Based on what you know about the family, do you think it is possible to arrive at a consensus around giving?

    _____

    _____

13. Irrespective of consensus, should resources be made available for each individual to give and to use as he or she wishes?

    _____

    _____

14. What level of recognition and visibility interests you?

    _____

    _____

15. What level of risk tolerance do you have? (That is, are these funds to be used as seed capital, or are you more interested in building organizational capacity within existing organizations?)

    _____

16. In which geographical range are you most interested in giving help: local, national, global, or some combination of all three?

_____

_____

17. Are you more interested in helping individuals or organizations, or do you wish to affect public policy?

_____

_____

18. Any other ideas or thoughts?

_____

_____

A Look at Three Family Challenges

I. Financial Inheritance as a Family Conversation

"I used to think I was up against more than I actually am regarding our daughters' inheritances," says Bill Collatos '76, founding managing partner of Spectrum Equity Investors in Boston. "The dialogue between my wife and me has taken an interesting turn. For some time, we had differences about how much to give our three daughters, but, after a few years and numerous conversations, we came up with the principles and the strategy, and then the dollar amounts came into sharper focus."

Several key questions illuminate decisions regarding a financial inheritance:

- What amount of financial inheritance will you leave for your children and grandchildren?

- What, if anything, will you tell your children about your estate plan and their inheritance? And, if you do tell them about this, how much detail will you provide?

- Will you actively help this next generation learn about finance and investments?

- Should you include sons- and daughters-in-law in these conversations?

- What do you think is the purpose of a financial inheritance for your children? For example, is it to be used to provide a safety net, to purchase a vacation home, to fund financial or social entrepreneurial initiatives, to enable a choice of career without regard for the economics of that choice, or for anything your children choose?

Because I believe that the true wealth of your family is not financial, I think that you should first discuss the *principles* that will guide your decision about how much to give your children. It makes sense to have these conversations *before* implementing various estate planning strategies. Remember, money is important, but not all-important. The best thing you can do for your family is to invest in their human, intellectual, and social capital.

"The most important truths, I believe," says Jay Hughes, a retired counselor of law in Aspen, Colorado, and the author of *Family Wealth—Keeping It in the Family*, "are whether the gifts will permit the recipient to bring his or her own dream to life and enable him or her the choice of a vocation. The priority is to help this person whom you love and invest in their journey. Another truth is that, if the recipient receives a greater sum than they need to live a liberated life, that extra sum will require them to act as a steward of those funds—for someone or something other than themselves. Those excess funds will impose a responsibility upon them that will restrict the experience of enhancement of freedom that the gift was designed to achieve."

What is the best way to proceed?

"Where should a parent begin?" asks Kathy Wiseman, a family facilitator and the CEO of Working Systems, Inc. "Should you begin with your spouse or your adult children? As with any discussion about a sensitive topic, it is important that all conversations about family assets be planned, factual and detail-based, open, and inviting of questions. Difficult conversations are always challenging, but the benefits are significant. Planning and thinking through what you want to achieve are a first step, while at the same time remembering that questions are a good start to knowing what it is that the next generation wants to learn."

My recommended process is a three-part conversation, starting with your spouse and then your children. One way through those questions listed previously is a series of "breakthrough conversations," which are critical to the success of the family in the future. The conversations start small and evolve over time.

The first part begins with a conversation with your spouse and focuses on exploring all your options. How much to give, through which vehicles— that is, outright or via trusts—etc. From that conversation, a key goal is to create clarity about what the inheritance should achieve and generally how much to leave the children. You may not agree, but differences are critically important and should be discussed and respected. Indeed, you may find that there are differences where you thought there were none, and points of agreement that you did not expect.

Ask yourselves the following questions:

- What principles guide our decisions regarding our children's inheritances? What factors might make it difficult to follow our principles?

- Do we treat our children equally or fairly? What are the challenges and solutions for both scenarios?

- At what stage do we tell them about their financial inheritance?

- What would our parents say about the financial inheritance we plan to leave our children?

- What worries us most about our children's use of their inheritances?

- What are our hopes for the next and then future generations?

- What amount of inheritance would be life-giving to our children?

- Could we give them a say in their financial inheritance?

The second part of the conversation is talking with your children about what you have decided in part one. You can have this talk with one child at a time or all the children together. Sometimes, families need only one conversation. Other families have a number of conversations, often over a number of years.

You may want to begin with the following general questions, with the option of adding others that are more specific to your own family:

- What is the meaning and purpose of a financial inheritance for you?

- How much money do you need to live a worthwhile life?

- What do you think about the purpose of inheritance for your generation?

- Do you want to bring your husband/wife/partner into this conversation?

- What is the best financial decision you have made? The worst?

- Is it important to you to work together with your siblings around inheritances?

- What are the challenges that your parents' estate presents for you and your family?

- What kind of guidance/consultation would assist you in the management of your parents' estate?

The third part of the conversation should be a discussion of the principles that guided your decisions, the general nature of the estate plan, and then the amounts that your children will receive. Also, you can explain how you have integrated some of their ideas into your planning. You can also discuss any next steps and other issues that focus on the future.

My primary message is this: **Think carefully about the purpose of the financial inheritance. Engage all of your children in conversations about your financial wealth and their inheritances.**

Planning for a financial inheritance is both a legal process and a family process. It is an opportunity for connection, education, and openness. It also can be an opportunity for strengthening the family as you address difficult issues with candor and respect.

"My wife and I are both comfortable with our decisions to date," says Bill Collatos, "but we view this as an iterative process. We have not told our daughters what we have done yet, but we will have a conversation when the last one graduates from college."

II. Prenuptial Arrangements as a Family Conversation

"My wife and I talked to our two daughters about a prenuptial arrangement when they were in college," says Steve Baird '74, president and CEO of a family business, Baird & Warner, a real estate company in Chicago. "After a number of conversations, they agreed to have a prenuptial arrangement when they get married. Our business has been good to the family for five generations, and I hope that the enterprise will survive another generation."

There are compelling arguments for having prenuptial arrangements for members of a family for whom a business is important. The company is a family asset and ongoing enterprise that may have been in place for a number of generations, and many families want to see the business continue to grow for many additional generations. A business family's financial future is interconnected in a way that is different from a financial family, whose worth may consist of houses and marketable securities that allow each member to manage his or her own financial affairs independently of the others. In contrast, having a vital business requires an interdependence among family members that is best served without competing outside interests of nonblood relatives or possible divorce disagreements.

If you have a family business or financial wealth or a vacation home that you would like to be part of your family's legacy in the future, should you consider a prenuptial arrangement for your children? Are you concerned that the dissolution of a marriage of one of the next generation heirs would jeopardize that cohesive ownership? If yes, what would make it feasible to talk with your children about a possible financial contract? Should you have *all* the children in the room? The primary question is, how do you prepare yourself for this important conversation? This can be an extremely difficult but rewarding conversation to have with your children.

Many families have had prenuptial arrangements and they often say to their children, "This is just what our family does." Other families stress that the financial wealth of the family is an important family asset and needs to be passed down for more than one generation. And the threat to that happening is worth planning for and discussing. In some cases, parents say that this takes money off the table when a young man or woman marries into your family—meaning that they are not marrying your son or daughter for their money. Some parents say to their daughter or son, "Your spouse will enjoy the benefits of our money for a long time." While these answers suffice at the start of the conversation, they do little to address the main issue and to use the opportunity to discuss an important topic with the next generation.

There is no question that timing about this conversation regarding prenuptial arrangements as an opportunity creates anxiety. This is an important and sensitive subject. There will be differences that provoke emotions. "Discussing them creates a lot of anxiety," says Michael Fay JD '75, senior partner in the Private Client Group of Wilmer Hale, a law firm in Boston. "The anxiety relates to the fact that these arrangements are intended to deal specifically with the possibility that the marriage will be terminated. Prenuptial arrangements have distrust written all over them. There is really no easy way to address this except by urging openness and honesty on both parties."

Another way of discussing a form of prenuptial arrangements can be started while talking about the trust documents and the financial legacy currently in place. Many parents have trusts for their children, and, in many cases, the parents think of the trust almost as a prenuptial arrangement. Some lawyers will say that the prenuptial arrangement is a companion document to reinforce the trust provisions for their children. Research indicates that a high percentage of what the children who are beneficiaries receive comes to them under discretionary trusts, and they have no control over the principal or the income during their lifetime.

At the root of the discussion is "the parents' fear as the driving force," says Jay Hughes, a retired counselor of law in Aspen and author of *Family Wealth— Keeping It in the Family*. "They are afraid of the money getting into the wrong hands, which often means their son-in-law who is not good enough. It is totally impractical to ask these young people to enter into an agreement requested by the earlier generation. The reason for doing this is the parents' fears—fears over financial assets that their children will never own." Perhaps articulating the fears in a conversation will assist in finding an agreeable solution.

Hughes continues his thinking: "The core question is, 'Can you be a resource to this young couple?' Can you have a conversation about money and discover one another's philosophy, so that whatever agreement emerges will reflect that philosophy? The highest good that parents should keep in mind is being focused on encouraging the success and sustainability of their children's relationships."

It is my opinion that one way through this prenuptial dilemma is a series of conversations that I call "breakthrough conversations." The topic of pre-nuptial agreements is hard to discuss and can be uncomfortable. It takes time and courage to confront. Needless to say, I think the conversation should take place early enough so that no fiancé(e) has yet arrived at the door.

My preferred process is a two-part conversation.

The first part begins with your spouse and focuses on what is impor-tant to you around your money and a prenuptial arrangement. A key goal is to create clarity about your expectations and why they are important to you. The two of you may not agree, but these differences should be discussed and respected. Indeed, you may find that there are differences where you thought there were none, and points of agreement that you did not expect.

Ask yourselves the following questions:

- What is the prenuptial arrangement meant to accomplish?
  For what reasons do you want a prenuptial arrangement?

- What worries you if your children get divorced?

- What history and principles inform your thinking around the prenuptial arrangement?

- Where have you seen this done well? Where have you seen it managed poorly?

- What would your parents say about asking your children to negotiate a prenuptial agreement?

- How does your faith factor into these decisions?

- What will it take to bring your children into a conversation around the idea of a prenuptial arrangement?

- What are the downsides of a prenuptial arrangement?

- Could you let the couple or the individual family member make their own decision?

- In what ways do you want to share some of your wealth with your daughter- or son-in-law?

The second part is a talk with your children about a prenuptial arrangement. You can have this talk one child at a time or with all the children together. It may be helpful to have a facilitator at one of your meetings. Steve Baird had a number of conversations with his daughters, and I led one discussion for the whole family.

Here are questions that you may want to ask:

- What is the purpose of the inheritance for the next generation?

- In what ways is a prenuptial arrangement important to you or not? Why?

- How do you differ from your mother or father?

- How do you differ from your siblings?

- Can you maintain separate financial resources and have a viable marriage? What would it take?

- What principles inform your thinking?

- What potential obstacles stand in the way of negotiating a prenuptial arrangement?

- How does your faith factor into these decisions?

- Could you bring your fiancé(e) into the conversation?

- What would your fiancé(e) be "up against" in marrying into our family?

- What are you "up against" in marrying into your fiancé(e)'s family?

- What is your dream for the future of your family?

So my suggestion is: **Engage all of your young adult children in conversations about the distribution of your financial wealth.** Planning for a possible prenuptial arrangement is both a legal process and a family process. Meaningful conversations over a period of time can be an opportunity for strengthening the family and addressing difficult topics with openness and respect. In the long run, these "breakthrough conversations" can be enormously informative and useful all around.

III. Stepfamilies: Who Gets the Money?

"Stepfamily inheritances are a very complex issue," says Peter Solomon '60, MBA '63. "It's an ongoing conversation and I don't have all of the answers."

Solomon, chairman of Peter J. Solomon Company, L. P., an investment banking advisory firm in New York City, has thought deeply about inheritances for the next generation. He has also taken a stand for the principle of equality of distributions made during his lifetime. He makes current gifts to his children, his wife's children, and all of their grandchildren in equal amounts. In his estate plan, he leaves money to his children and to his wife, both to secure her financial position and to support her charitable giving.

Estate planning for stepfamilies represents a complicated transition. It is hard enough to bring two families together, but when there is money of consequence, competing claims often arise. All families are unique and there is no route to follow as a stepfamily. Typically, one or both spouses bring children from a previous marriage, and sometimes they have a child together.

"There are a number of planning challenges for stepfamilies," says Nancy B. Gardiner '78, director of Select Client Services at Hemenway & Barnes, a law firm in Boston. "The problems vary, based on the age of the parents, the nature of their holdings, and the ages of their children. In the midst of the joy of a second marriage, significant questions are often lurking."

Who, then, receives a financial inheritance? The wealthier spouse usually wants to provide for his or her second spouse, even though he or she may still be making alimony payments. But a number of difficult questions emerge. What will the wealthy father's children think if they have to wait for the younger second wife to die before they receive a financial inheritance? In a long-term marriage, do the children of the less wealthy stepdad expect an inheritance from their wealthier stepmom? If you want to provide an inheritance to your stepchildren, what would be an appropriate amount vis-à-vis your own children? How do you factor in the potential inheritances from an ex-spouse? What are you—as a stepfamily—up against in making a decision?

One way through these dilemmas is a series of conversations that we might call "breakthrough conversations." Some topics are hard to discuss and can be uncomfortable. It takes time and courage to confront these issues.

"A thoughtful estate plan for stepparents," says Gardiner, "results when there is an opportunity for an open conversation among family members."

My preferred process is a three-part conversation.

The first part begins with your spouse and focuses on your options. A key goal is to create clarity about your expectations of how much to leave the children—both yours and your spouse's—if anything. You may not agree, but these differences should be discussed and respected. Indeed, you may find that there are differences where you thought there were none, and points of agreement that you did not expect.

Ask yourselves the following questions:

- How do you think about sharing some of your wealth with your second spouse and his or her children?

- What is the inheritance meant to accomplish?

- What principles inform your thinking?

- Where have you seen inheritances in a stepfamily managed well?

- Where have you seen them managed poorly?

- What worries you if your children have to wait for a financial inheritance because of your second marriage?

- What would your parents say about these decisions?

- Can you bring your children and stepchildren into the conversation?

The second part is a talk with your children and your second spouse's children to get their impressions. You may be able to bring both sets of children together for this important conversation. Remember, it is your responsibility to make these decisions, but giving your children a "say" can be an important contribution to making a truly thoughtful decision.

Here are four questions to ask the next generation:

- How did you adapt to the second marriage of your father/mother?

- What are your expectations for a financial inheritance?

- How do you differ on that question from your siblings and your stepsiblings?

- How do you view the purpose of an inheritance from your stepmom/stepdad?

In the third discussion, you tell all of the children about your decision regarding your estate plan, why it is important to you, and how you integrated some of their ideas into it. You can also discuss any next steps and other topics that focus on the future.

Here is my suggestion: **Engage all of your adult children and stepchildren in a conversation.** Estate planning for stepfamilies is both a legal process and a family process. A central tool for the family process is a number of meaningful discussions held over time. In the long run, these breakthrough conversations could be transformative.

"I'm giving as much money as possible to my children while I'm living," says Peter Solomon. "The benefit in telling my children what they have and can expect is that they can plan a life within the parameters of that money. This is important to me because it fosters their independence and encourages them to lead their own lives."

APPENDIX D

Additional Resources

Association of Small Foundations
1720 N Street NW
Washington, DC 20036
(202) 580-6560
www.smallfoundations.org

Council on Foundations
1828 L Street NW, Suite 300
Washington, DC 20036
(202) 466-6512
www.cof.org

Family Firm Institute
200 Lincoln Street
Boston, MA 02111
(617) 482-3045
www.ffi.org

Family Office Exchange
100 S. Wacker Drive
Chicago, IL 60606
(312) 327-1200
www.familyoffice.com

First Foundation Advisors
18101 Von Karman Avenue, Suite 700
Irvine, CA 92612-0145
(800) 224-7931
(949) 833-1112
www.ff-inc.com

Independent Means, Inc.
126 E. Haley Street
Santa Barbara, CA 93101
(805) 965-0475
www.independentmeans.com

Institute for Private Investors
17 State Street, 5th Floor
New York, NY 10004
(212) 693-1300
www.memberlink.net

National Center for Family Philanthropy
1818 N Street, NW
Washington, DC 20036
(202) 293-3424
www.ncfp.org

National Family Business Council
Private Family Advisor™
1640 W. Kennedy Road
Lake Forest, IL 60045
(847) 295-1040
www.privatefamilyadvisor.com

The Philanthropic Initiative
160 Federal Street, 8th Floor
Boston, MA 02110
(617) 338-2590
www.tpi.org

The Philanthropy Workshop West
2121 Sand Hill Road
Menlo Park, CA 94025
(650) 234-4691
www.tpwwest.org

Relative Solutions
764 Ashbury Street
San Francisco, CA 94117
(414) 665-8699
www.relative-solutions.com

Rockefeller Philanthropy Advisors
437 Madison Avenue
New York, NY 10022-7001
(212) 812-4330
www.rockpa.org

Wealthbridge Partners
2201 Wisconsin Avenue NW, Suite 333
Washington, DC 20007
(202) 333-1963
www.wealthbridgepartners.com

Working Systems
4545 42nd Street, NW, Suite 201
Washington, DC 20016
(202) 244-6481
www.workingsystemsinc.net

Bibliography

Esposito, Virginia M., Editor. (2002). *Splendid Legacy*. National Center for Family Philanthropy.

Gallo, E. and Gallo, J. (2005). *The Financially Intelligent Parent: 8 Steps to Raising Successful, Generous, Responsible Children*. New York: New American Library.

Gersick, K. E. (2004). *Generations of Giving*. Lanham, MD: Lexington Books.

Gilbert, R. M. *Connecting with Our Children*. New York: John Wiley & Sons, Inc.

Gilbert, R. M. (1992). *Extraordinary Relationships: A New Way of Thinking About Human Interactions*. New York: John Wiley & Sons, Inc.

Gillis, J. R. (1996). *A World of Our Own Making: Myth, Ritual, and the Quest for Family Values*. Cambridge, MA: Harvard University Press.

Godfrey, J. (2003). *Raising Financially Fit Kids*. Berkeley, CA: Ten Speed Press.

Hausner, L. (2005). *Children of Paradise: Successful Parenting for Prosperous Families*. Irvine, CA: Plaza Press.

Hollander, Stuart J. (2007). *Saving the Family Cottage*. Suttons Bay, MI: Pleasant City Press, LLC.

Hughes, J. E., Jr. (2004). *Family Wealth: Keeping It in the Family*. Princeton, NJ: Bloomberg Press.

Jaffe, D. T. (1991). *Working with the Ones You Love: Strategies for a Successful Family Business*. San Francisco: Aspen Family Business Group.

Kegan, R. (1994). *In Over Our Heads: The Mental Demands of Modern Life*. Cambridge, MA: Harvard University Press.

Lansberg, I. (1999). *Succeeding Generations: Realizing the Dream of Families in Business*. Cambridge, MA: Harvard Business School Press.

McGoldrick, Monica (1995). *You Can Go Home Again: Reconnecting with Your Family*. New York: W. W. Norton & Company.

Williamson, D. S. (1991). *The Intimacy Paradox: Personal Authority in the Family System*. New York: The Guilford Press.

Charles W. Collier

Charles W. Collier retired in December 2011 as the senior philanthropic adviser at Harvard University. He is a nationally recognized expert on planned giving, family philanthropy, and family wealth advising. Collier has also served Phillips Academy, Andover; Dartmouth College; Brown University; and Princeton University. He is a senior fellow at The Philanthropic Initiative, Inc., is on the board of the Family Foundation Advisor, and is a member of the Committee on the Emotional and Psychological Issues in Estate Planning of the American Bar Association. Collier has published articles in *Trusts & Estates*, the *ACTEC Journal*, *Family Business Review*, the *Journal of Gift Planning*, *Advancing Philanthropy*, and *Gift Planning Today*. He has been quoted in the *Boston Globe*, *New York Times*, *Wall Street Journal*, *Financial Times*, and *Forbes*. The *Chronicle of Philanthropy* featured his work in an article entitled "Gaining a Family's Trust," and he was also named to *The NonProfit Times* Power & Influence Top 50. Over the past 35 years, Collier has worked with hundreds of individuals and families to help them think through the questions addressed in this book. He graduated from Phillips Academy, Andover, and holds an AB in Religion from Dartmouth College and an MTS from Harvard Divinity School.

Inquiries about *Wealth in Families* should be directed to Harvard's current philanthropic adviser, Alasdair H. Halliday.

alasdair_halliday@harvard.edu | 617-496-6957